50 FINDS FROM CHILDHOOD

OBJECTS FROM THE PORTABLE ANTIQUITIES SCHEME

Kayt Hawkins

AMBERLEY

First published 2024

Amberley Publishing
The Hill, Stroud
Gloucestershire, GL5 4EP

www.amberley-books.com

Copyright © Kayt Hawkins, 2024

The right of Kayt Hawkins to be identified as the
Author of this work has been asserted in accordance
with the Copyrights, Designs and Patents Act 1988.

ISBN 978 1 3981 1485 2 (print)
ISBN 978 1 3981 1486 9 (ebook)

British Library Cataloguing in Publication Data.
A catalogue record for this book is available from
the British Library.

Typeset in 10pt on 13pt Celeste.
Typesetting by SJmagic DESIGN SERVICES, India.
Printed in the UK.

Contents

Acknowledgements

This book features fifty finds from England and Wales recorded by the Portable Antiquities Scheme (PAS) up to May 2023. It could not have been written without the co-operation of members of the public who have provided their finds for recording and the subsequent records created by the PAS Finds Liaison Officers (FLOs). Several years ago, I had the privilege of sharing an office with David Wynn Williams, then FLO for Surrey, who introduced me to the PAS. I wish to thank all the FLOs, Finds Assistants and members of the public whose records form the basis of this book, and those who have helped answer my subsequent queries.

I also wish to thank those within and beyond my professional networks, whose friendship, comments and advice has been so valuable, particular thanks are due to Tess Machling, Louise Rayner and Katie Hinds. Any errors of course remain my own. As a piece of unfunded work this could also not have been written without the patience and support of my husband, my children and wider family members who have endured its constant presence, influencing family days out and holiday destinations, lost weekends and countless late nights. I am incredibly grateful for their unwavering love in accepting this invasion of family time.

Within the book, each object has been presented along with its unique identifier which enables the object to be located on the PAS database; for most objects more detailed descriptive information and further images are located on the original record. Unless otherwise stated, the images used herein are courtesy of the Portable Antiquities Scheme under Creative Commons by Attribution licence (2.0 and 4.0). Various organisations have also supplied images and granted permissions, including The Vindolanda Trust, Herefordshire Museums Service, Carisbrooke Castle Museum, Potted History and Museum of London Archaeology. Every attempt has been made to seek permission for copyrighted material used in this book, and any inadvertently used without permission and acknowledgement will be corrected at the first opportunity.

Foreword

The places in which we live and work have a long past, but one that is not always obvious in the landscape around us. This is a forgotten past. Most of us know little about the people who once lived in our communities fifty years ago, let alone 500, or even 5,000 years past. Like us, they lived, played and worked here, in this place, but we know almost nothing of them.

History books tell us about royalty, great lords and important churchmen, but most others are forgotten by time. The only evidence for many of these people is the objects that they left behind; sometimes buried on purpose, but more often lost by chance. Occasionally, through archaeological fieldwork, we can place these objects in a context that allows us to better understand the past, but nowadays excavation is mostly development-led, so only takes place when a new building, road or service pipe, is being constructed.

A unique way of understanding the past is through the finds recorded through the Portable Antiquities Scheme, and those chosen here by Kayt Hawkins are fifty finds from its database (www.finds.org.uk). These finds are all discovered by the public, most by metal-detector users, searching in places archaeologists are unlikely to go or otherwise excavate. As such they provide important clues of underlying archaeology that, once recorded, help archaeologists understand our past – a past of the people, found by the people.

Some of these finds are truly magnificent, others less imposing. Yet, like pieces in a jigsaw puzzle they are often meaningless alone, but once placed together paint a picture. These finds therefore allow us to understand the story of people who once lived here, in Britain.

Dr Michael Lewis
Head of Portable Antiquities & Treasure
British Museum

Chapter 1
Childhood Objects from the Portable Antiquities Scheme

What do we mean by 'childhood' when looking at the past, when for a large expanse of human existence we have no firm evidence of how it might have been perceived or experienced? The current definition of childhood, as stated by the United Nations Convention on the Rights of the Child (UNCRC), includes everyone under the age of 18 unless, 'under the law applicable to the child, majority is attained earlier'. Any concept of childhood, however, has varied considerably across time and place, at any one point being a complicated mix of cultural expectations, within which the individual lived experience of a young person could have varied significantly depending on their family situation. In this book, the term childhood is, therefore, used broadly to relate to the time in an individual's life between infancy and adolescence.

In brief, evidence for any childhood experience in prehistoric Britain is elusive. However, following the arrival of the Romans in the mid-first century AD we start to have a clearer understanding of how Roman attitudes to children may have influenced, or been integrated into, the established population. Roman approaches to what we would consider 'childhood' were formalised into clear stages. High mortality rates meant children were not given a name at birth but several days later (day eight for girls, day nine for boys), after which a ceremony (*dies lustricus*) formally welcomed them into the family. At this ceremony the child was given a protective amulet (boys were given a *bulla* and girls a *lunula*) to wear until adulthood, which was reached at the age of twelve for girls and fourteen for boys. Children over the age of eight could be found guilty of crimes, although the punishments were usually mild. In tenth-century England children from the age of twelve were tried as adults, with all the punishments that could entail.

While ideas about childhood may have changed during the medieval period, a 'childhood' phase was very much experienced and can be evidenced through documents, art and material objects. In England during the sixteenth century there were numerous societal changes that impacted on children specifically, such as the introduction in 1598 of the Poor Relief Act, through which poor children became the responsibility of individual parishes. This Act paved the way for much of the late nineteenth-century legislation regarding children and education which affected much of the population of Victorian Britain.

Whereas other works that have explored material recorded by the PAS have focused on specific geographical areas, chronological periods (for example *50 Roman Finds*) or find types (*50 Medieval Coins*), to which the PAS data lends itself very well, this volume takes a slightly different approach by exploring a wide range of artefacts linked by the common theme of childhood.

This has not been as straightforward a task as it may sound. While objects for the care of children are perhaps more easily identifiable in the archaeological record, those relating to play can be more obscure. Children are adept at utilising any manner of materials in creative play, and for archaeologists these can be near impossible to recognise. Even a stick can be anything from a sword to a hobby horse, if that is the role demanded. In identifying fifty finds from childhood within the PAS records, care has been taken not to impose modern expectations in interpretation, particularly for earlier periods where there is less certainty; size does not always matter in that small or miniature objects, for example, do not automatically imply use for or by children.

Although the PAS database is undoubtedly a valuable resource, due to the nature of the evidence recorded it is important to recognise its limitations. With its remit to record objects discovered by members of the public, many of whom are metal-detectorists, there is a bias towards metal, although ceramic, stone and glass are also recorded. Items made from organic materials, such as textiles relating to swaddling and clothing, due to their poor preservation are absent. There are also biases inherent in what the public, archaeologists and curators consider to be of importance and worth recording, particularly when it comes to relatively modern objects. The inclusion on the database of objects of more recent date is largely down to the discretion of the individual FLO, and this can in part be seen in the selection of objects in this book. In choosing these objects it is also noted that there is

Table: Agreed Date Ranges for the Broad Periods Used When Recording Objects on the Portable Antiquities Scheme

Time Period on the PAS	Date Range
Palaeolithic	500,00–10,001 BC
Mesolithic	10,000–4001 BC
Neolithic	4000–2351 BC
Bronze Age	2350–801 BC
Iron Age	800 BC–AD 42
Roman	AD 43–409
Early Medieval	AD 410–1066
Medieval	AD 1066–1539
Post-medieval	AD 1540–1900
Modern	AD 1901–Present

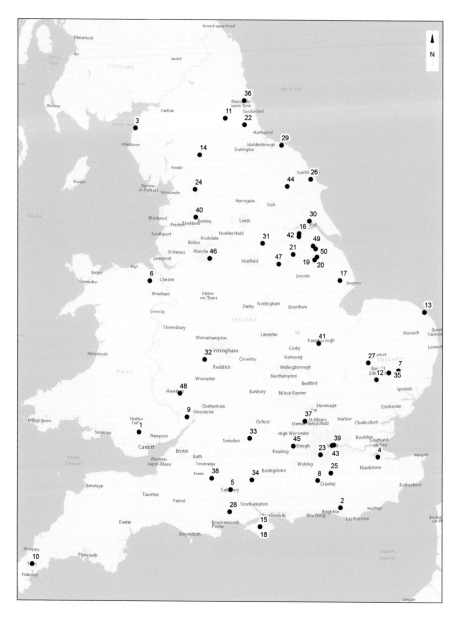

Map showing the locations of the fifty finds selected. (Fiona Griffin)

considerable discrepancy in the amount of material recorded under different chronological time periods, with material from the post-medieval period vastly outweighing that of the earlier periods.

While following the traditional format of the 50 Finds series, this book attempts to address this last bias by using the individual find as an introduction, and where possible providing supplementary evidence of earlier examples from other collections. A number of objects within this book have long histories and are yet still familiar to a modern audience.

Chapter 2
Everyday Care

This first section looks at objects recorded by the PAS that reflect aspects of everyday health and well-being for mother and child. Following pregnancy and birth, the basic needs of newborns are universal and include cleaning, clothing, feeding, comforting and entertaining. Despite the recovery biases already identified in the PAS dataset, there are several individual objects that show how contemporary societies met these practical needs. In addition, the figurines and votive offerings on the database are an insight into the hopes and wishes of expectant mothers, after all, for most of human history pregnancy has been a time of vulnerability and danger for women.

Archaeologists working on the 'Motherhood in Prehistory' project are revealing many aspects of child-rearing and challenging previous assumptions. For the classical period we have writings from many contemporary physicians, for example, the following quote from Galen of Pergamon, writing in the second century AD:

> If it is not clear what they [babies] want and meanwhile the demand is becoming more urgent, let things be put right by immediately giving whatever is needed and so prevent their becoming exhausted. In the meantime by rocking in the arms and lullabies, such as the more experienced nurses use, one may seek to soothe them.

Historical writings also show that modern conversations around the 'best' way to feed infants are nothing new, with conflicting advice from Roman physicians over the benefits of colostrum and when and what to feed babies. Breastfeeding may have been viewed as best, but women from wealthy families were encouraged to use wet-nurses, a practice that continued across all social classes throughout the medieval and post-medieval periods.

Due to the general poor survival of wood and textiles in archaeological contexts in Britain, many everyday objects of childhood do not make it onto the PAS database. An example, therefore, of evidence missing in these records is the swaddling of infants, which has a long history in infant care of keeping babies both safe (immobile) and warm as well as it being believed to help protect bone growth. Swaddled babies could be carried via a sling or cradleboard or placed in a separate crib or cradle to sleep and be kept safe. Co-sleeping is still controversial today, as it was in the medieval period, with at least one fourteenth-century writer advising against the practice purely because children would prefer it to sleeping on their own. Historical sources, such as documents and artwork, show that some of the equipment on today's parents' wish lists were also in use during the sixteenth and seventeenth centuries, for example, walking frames and high-chairs.

There is no doubt that childhood was tough in the past, and despite a parent's best efforts, the first years of life were dangerous, with mortality rates as high as 30 to 50 per cent from prehistory through to the early twentieth century in Britain. As sad as this evidence is for a modern reader, it also provides important information on childhood, for example, through the details on Roman funerary monuments and inscriptions, and the many medieval court papers which shed light on the daily activities of young children and the perils inherent therein. The mourning jewellery included in this section provides a potent reminder that death was no stranger to children in the past.

Roman coin of the Empress Theodora (*c.* AD 337–40) showing the deity Pietas who is carrying an infant. This imagery represents Theodora fulfilling her Roman duty as a good mother. (OXON-EC1C26)

Medieval lead-alloy spoon fragment showing swaddled infant on one side, elongated adult face on the other. (NLM-DC3483)

Child's high-chair, British *c*. AD 1660. (Image courtesy of the Metropolitan Museum of Art)

1. Sandstone pebble 'Venus' figurine (PUBLIC-0ADB67)
Post-medieval (AD 1700–1900)
Found at Abercynon, Rhondda Cynon Taf. Length 144.6 mm, weight 730.4 g
Identified and recorded by a member of the public.

Depictions of the female body in many different materials, including clay, stone and wood, have been found across the globe and from the Palaeolithic Age to the modern period. Often particular body parts are exaggerated, such as breasts and belly, which has led researchers to view these as somehow connected to fertility and pregnancy, although more recently other interpretations have been put forward. The examples probably most familiar to people are the Upper Palaeolithic 'Venus' figurines, named by archaeologists after the Greco-Roman goddess of love because at the time they believed these wonderfully voluptuous figurines must have been related to sex in some way.

This carved sandstone pebble is one of a group of similar pebbles found in 1939. These are very portable, tactile objects, and the suspension hole present on some would suggest they could have been worn, perhaps as an amulet (PUBLIC-0B1D47). A lack of context makes dating problematic and some aspects of the carving would suggest a probable post-medieval or later date. The discovery of these objects during works at the Cynon River could be significant as watery places have often been associated with depositing or offering valuable items. If they are of nineteenth- or twentieth-century date, then they could be an example of the merging of folklore, mythology and more recent goddess movements. After, all folklore surrounding the power inherent in fertility and pregnancy has a long history, as does the repurposing of ancient artefacts and imbuing them with varied and complex new meanings. A good example of this could also be the second figurine shown here, carved from quartz; white quartz pebbles have been found in prehistoric graves and also have an association in Irish folklore with the fairy people of Si.

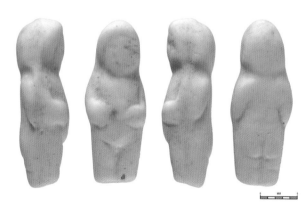

Above: Quartz anthropomorphic figurine, *c.* AD 1500–1900, length 22.4 mm. (PUBLIC-923677)

Left: Sandstone 'Venus' figurine. (PUBLIC-0ADB67)

2. Votive plaque (SUSS-0F1783)
Roman (AD 43–410)
Found in Lewes, East Sussex. Length c. 30.84 mm, weight 1.85 g
Identified and recorded by Stephanie Smith with Martin Henig.

For most of history, fertility and childbirth have been precarious aspects of women's lives, while the source of much interest to men. In the Roman world, physicians such as Pliny the Elder and Soranus of Ephesus wrote extensively on matters of fertility, conception, pregnancy, childbirth and infant care – it was, after all, the duty of Roman women to provide children. The PAS database contains two examples of divine intervention being called on for help. A votive object is one that has been dedicated to a deity through a vow or promise, often displayed or left at a religious or sacred site. Roman votive objects representing just about every body part are known from across the Roman Empire, but they are not common finds in Britain, being usually associated with temple sites. This gold uterus votive plaque (in two parts that fit together) is thought to be a unique find in Britain. Gold, in addition to being an expensive commodity, was also believed to possess magical properties as a metal of the gods, and to be particularly effective against various illnesses, so this would have been seen as a particularly powerful object. It is not possible to say what the desired outcome was from dedicating this object, although it could have been to ensure either fertility or success in childbirth. Fear for loved ones regarding childbirth are expressed in a second votive plaque or phylactery, composed of several lines of writing expressing a mother's hope for her daughter's pregnancy (BERK-0B671 2007TI), which would have been rolled up and worn in a case, possibly as a necklace.

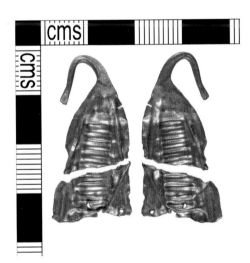  

Above left: Roman gold-leaf votive uterus in two parts. (SUSS-0F1783)

Above middle: Roman clay votive offering in the shape of a uterus. (Image courtesy of the Wellcome Collection. Attribution 4.0 International (CC BY 4.0))

Above right: Roman gold phylactery inscribed with several lines of writing, c. AD 200–300, length 63 mm. (BERK-0B6771)

13

3. Dea Nutrix figurine (LANCUM-9670B3)
Roman (AD 100–200)
Found at Maryport, Cumbria. Height 107 mm, weight 148.62 g
Identified and recorded by Faye Simpson.

Dea Nutrix figurines show a goddess sat in a high-backed wicker chair, breastfeeding either one or two infants. These figures have been found across Britain, although they originate in Roman Gaul (an area covering modern-day France, parts of Belgium, Western Germany and Northern Italy) where they were mass-produced in moulds from pipeclay. Although rare finds in Britain, with the examples recorded on the database being incomplete, other examples have been found intact and can be seen, for example, at Canterbury Museum. The fact that they are broken, however, may be significant and is thought to have been a deliberate act, possibly ritual. The Romans were known for merging local deities with those of Rome, for example Sulis-Minerva at Bath, and it is possible that these figures represent a Celtic mother-type goddess with the Roman goddess Juno Lucina, who was closely linked to motherhood. Portrayals of breastfeeding occur often in Roman art, although Roman women, particularly those from wealthy families, were encouraged to use wet-nurses rather than breastfeed their own children.

Above left: Incomplete Dea Nutrix figurine. (LANCUM-9670B3)

Above right: Replica of a Dea Nutrix figurine found at the site of the Roman settlement Margidunum, near Nottingham. (Image courtesy of Potted History)

4. Infant feeding vessel (*tettine*) (PUBLIC-FF0848)
Roman (AD 50–200)
Found in Upchurch, Kent. Height 71.94 mm, weight 136 g
Identified and recorded by Wendy Thompson.

Continuing the theme of infant feeding, where breastfeeding wasn't an option for a Roman mother and no wet-nurses were available, these small, spouted pottery vessels may have been used as a form of Roman 'baby bottle'. Alternatively, they could have been used during weaning as a way of providing supplementary foodstuffs alongside breast milk, or to administer medicines. Roman doctors advised that babies should be given breast milk until three years old, although once they cut their first tooth, other foods could be given. Analysis of Roman skeletons from London have shown that babies were indeed weaned from around six months old on cereal-based food, possibly not unlike the baby rice products available today.

These vessels are not common finds in Britain and do show a strong connection with babies and young infants, but also with the Roman military as they are often found in areas of Britain where the Roman army was present. As they also occur on the Continent, it may have been that families moving to Britain with the army brought this form of infant feeding with them. Alternative explanations for these vessels have included their use as invalid cups for soldiers, or even as lamp fillers. It is possible to use scientific methods to detect and identify traces of residues left from whatever had been held in pottery, and analysis of some prehistoric and Roman vessels has indeed shown evidence that they contained milk. The small perforation would have made drinking anything other than something watery quite hard work and keeping them clean would have been difficult. There is no evidence that these early bottles would have had any sort of teat over the spout, unlike much later Victorian examples which used rubber teats that were notoriously dangerous for accumulating bacteria.

Roman spouted vessel (*tettine*), made at
Upchurch, Kent. (PUBLIC-FF0848)

15

Child with feeding bottle. This woodcut appears in 'Ein Regiment ... für die jungen Kinder' by Heinrich von Louffenberg, published in 1539. (Wellcome Collection)

Infant's feeding bottle, rubber teats and box, *c.* 1850–99. (Wellcome Collection. Attribution 4.0 International (CC BY 4.0))

5. Child's spoon (WILT-884E90)
Medieval (AD 1066–1539)
Found in Salisbury, Wiltshire. Length 70.15 mm, weight 5.94 g
Identified and recorded by Alyson Tanner.

Spoon-feeding as a form of weaning is common today but may have a long history as experimental work on Neolithic spoons from Serbia has shown wear consistent with this practice. Roman doctors recommended introducing other foodstuffs to babies from around the age of six months, which is the same as modern-day guidance from the NHS. Recent studies from Scotland have shown that in the sixteenth and seventeenth centuries babies were also being weaned early, at the same time the practice of wet-nursing was becoming unpopular (at various points in the past people believed the characteristics of the wet-nurse could be transferred to the baby). By the seventeenth century a particular small spoon, known as a 'pap' spoon, was used for feeding young infants a gruel comprising milk and bread and for giving medicine to young children. Baby food in jars was introduced in the 1920s and before this, as is often the case today, babies would have eaten a variety of suitable foods, probably with their fingers. Spoons in silver and other metals are known in Britain from the Roman period, but these tended to be used by the wealthy in society. Spoons were also made of horn and wood, but these are rare survivals in the archaeological record. Those intended for children in the past can be difficult to identify, however, and the spoon selected here has also been described as a possible toy or apothecary's spoon. Another example on the database which could have been suitable for a child includes a bone spoon (LIN-2C8293).

Above: A bone spoon with shallow bowl, possibly for use with a child, *c.* AD 1700–1800. (LIN-2C8293)

Right: Copper-alloy medieval spoon. (WILT-884E90)

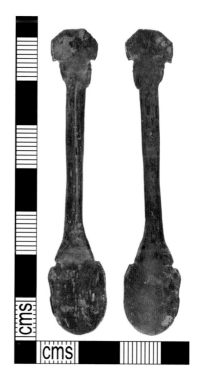

6. Bovril medal (WREX-6C725E)
Modern (AD 1886–1914)
Found in Gwernaffield, Flintshire. Length 33.7 mm, weight 3.18 g
Identified and recorded by Susie White.

Originally named Johnston's Fluid Beef, the concentrated beef extract created to supplement the rations of soldiers was re-named Bovril in 1886. Marketed for its health and nutritional benefits, Bovril was considered a 'superfood' in both world wars, was endorsed by the Pope, taken on expeditions to the North Pole and Everest, and became an institution as a hot drink at football matches. A further endeavour by Bovril was the creation of Virol, a sweet and sticky malt tonic that was a by-product of the brewing industry. It was introduced in 1899 and specifically aimed at providing extra nutrition, beyond that supplied by Bovril, for young children. In the 1940s, in exchange for a penny, schoolchildren would be given a weekly spoonful of Virol, which was advertised as essential for 'anaemic girls, growing boys and delicate children'. Virol was given a specific mention in 'Cornwall in Childhood', a poem by John Betjeman, British Poet Laureate (1972–84):

> Come, Hygiene, goddess of the growing boy,
> I here salute thee in Sanatogen!
> Anaemic girls need Virol, but for me
> Be Scott's Emulsion, rusks, and Mellin's Food,
> Cod-liver oil and malt, and for my neck
> Wright's Coal Tar Soap, Euthymol for my teeth.

On the PAS database there are several advertising tokens for Bovril, in addition to this promotional medal in the shape of the Victoria Cross, which states: '50 / TIMES / MORE NOURISHING / THAN / ORDINARY EXTRACT / OF MEAT / OR / BEEF'.

Above left: Promotional medal for Bovril. (WREX-6C725E)

Above right: Virol baby growth record book. (Image author's collection)

7. Pears Soap advertising token (SF-0195EA)
Modern (AD 1861–1900)
Found in Suffolk. Diameter 29.77 mm, weight 7.78 g
Identified and recorded by Alex Bliss.

Pears Soap was developed by Andrew Pears and first advertised in early nineteenth-century London. As a father of young children, he was concerned about the type of products that were being used on children, many of the available soaps being very harsh and often containing products now known to be poisonous, such as arsenic and lead. Pears claimed his soap was made by a 'curious chemical process by which soap is separated from all the impure and noxious substances'. Its translucent colour and appealing smell certainly made it stand out from its competitors. The addition to the Pears family, through marriage, of Thomas J. Barrett led to one of the most successful advertising campaigns ever, featuring iconic images such as 'Bubbles' and endorsement from the famous socialite Lillie Langtry. However, much of the Pears Soap advertising reflected racial stereotyping, explicitly racist but commonplace at the time. The *Pears Annual* was published between 1891 and 1925, and between 1959 and 1997 the winners of the Miss Pears Competition received a cash prize and their image was used in the advertising of Pears.

Another of Barrett's marketing tactics was the purchase, in the late nineteenth century, of thousands of Napoleonic coins which were over-stamped with the legend 'Pears Soap'. Two of these advertising tokens for Pears Soap have been recorded by the PAS, one of which is shown below.

Above: A copper-alloy advertising token for Pears Soap. (SF-0195EA)

Right: Advert for Pears Soap. (Wellcome Collection. Attribution 4.0 International (CC BY 4.0))

8. Child's leather shoe (SUR-B4C651)
Post-medieval (AD 1800–25)
Found at Ockley, Surrey. Length 20 mm, weight 238 g
Identified and recorded by Margaret Broomfield with Quita Mould.

The history of children's footwear is well documented in Britain, with both Roman and medieval examples recorded by archaeologists. Many children would have gone barefoot, even up to the mid-twentieth century, others would have worn footwear made of leather, other textiles or wood. Leather and organic materials do not usually survive well in archaeological contexts unless they are in waterlogged (anaerobic) conditions. At the Roman site of Vindolanda the preservation of leather and textiles is remarkable, and over 5,000 leather shoes have been recovered, including those of children. One of the most well known is a tiny baby boot that may have belonged to one of the children of Flavius Cerialis, an officer stationed at Vindolanda.

There is little evidence of children's clothing recorded by the PAS, except for a small number of Victorian children's leather shoes, two of which from Surrey have an interesting context. Both SUR-B4C651 and SUR-C78410 were found hidden within walls at different houses. The practice of placing objects within the walls of buildings, often near windows, doorways or chimneys, has a long tradition, with the earliest example of concealed shoes being those found at Winchester Cathedral, where they were placed behind the choir stalls in 1308. The placing of shoes may have been an act to ward off evil, or to bring good luck or protection to the inhabitants. Many parents keep their child's first pair of shoes, although these days mainly for sentimental rather than superstitious reasons (the author knows of someone in the 1960s who kept a pair of his son's baby shoes in his work van as a good-luck talisman). In the nineteenth century leather shoes were still an expensive item for many families, with children's shoes being repaired and passed onto the next child in the family, so there must have been a great deal of significance attached to taking a single shoe out of circulation.

Some of the most well-known children's footwear brands today have a long history. Start-Rite was founded in 1792 and Clarks in 1825, the latter being a driving force in the mass-production of children's footwear in the late 1800s.

Above: Roman leather baby boot imitating an adult style of shoe with fishnet upper. (Image copyright The Vindolanda Trust)

Left: Child's closed-tab, front-lacing leather boot, equivalent to a modern child's shoe size 12 for a child aged approximately six to eight years old. (SUR-B4C651)

9. Bronze Age children's bracelets (GLO-E9EC16)
Bronze Age (1500–1100 BC)
Found in the Forest of Dean, Gloucestershire. Diameter of four objects: B.1: 42 mm
by 40 mm; B.2: 39 mm by 35mm; B.3: 34 mm by 34 mm; B.4: 30 mm by 32 mm
Identified and recorded by Kurt Adams with Neil Wilkin.

Gold-working has been identified from around 2500 BC in Britain, at the end of the
Neolithic to early Bronze Age. One of the most well-known types of Bronze Age jewellery
is the torc, a band of metal (usually gold) twisted and shaped, sometimes decorated, and
made in various sizes to possibly be worn on different parts of the body. Other forms
of jewellery at this time include gorgets (flattened pieces of gold worn as neck collars),
bracelets, armlets and rings. The objects illustrated here are part of a remarkable hoard,
found deposited together in 'sets' of similar size and decoration. Under the Treasure Act
(1996) the gold objects are classed as Treasure as they are over 300 years old and contain
10 per cent or more of precious metal. Although it is not entirely clear how they may
have been worn, the use of hooked fastenings suggests they may have been bracelets, and
the small size of one set (Group B) indicates they could have been worn by children. We
don't have secure evidence to support this, other than the size of the bracelets, but further
examples, also possibly for children, have been recorded elsewhere across Britain, for
example, at Hillhead, Caithness, and Dawlish, Cornwall.

Three 'nested sets' of gold bracelets found as a hoard, Bronze Age. (GLO-E9EC16)

10. Gold ring (CORN-437A92)
Roman (AD 43–100)
Found in Cornwall. External diameter 16.2 mm, weight 1.2 g
Identified and recorded by Anna Tyacke.

For the Roman period, some jewellery we know from written sources was particularly related to children, for example the *bulla* worn by young boys and *lunula* pendant by girls for protection. We can be less certain about other forms of jewellery for children, except those from burials. The gold ring example shown here probably belonged to a child of between five and eight years old, and is decorated with a stylised palm branch, a common motif symbolising victory over death which also occurs on similar rings found in Germany and Italy. Also on the database, a gold bracelet (BM-C98DB9), which, with its simple hook-and-eye fastening, can be paralleled to a copper-alloy version found accompanying a child buried at York in the Roman period. Other bracelets found with children are made from jet or shale, although an unusual bracelet (KENT-0B1627) in a combination of gold and a mineral found in Germany called variscite probably came from the Continent where evidence of similar techniques and styles has been found.

Roman child's gold ring with stylised palm-branch decoration. (CORN-437A92)

Right: Roman gold and variscite bracelet, *c.* AD 225–75, length 132 mm. (KENT-0B1627)

Below: Roman *lunula* pendant, *c.* AD 43–410, dimensions 25.46 mm × 21.04 mm × 4.21 mm. (DOR-E3E5E4)

11. Lead doll (NCL-DB1E00)
Post-medieval (AD 1550–1600)
Found in Healeyfield, County Durham. Height 93.19 mm, weight 57.3 g
Identified and recorded by Robert Collins.

This lead doll can be dated through the style of clothing to the end of the Tudor period, which lasted from AD 1485 to 1603. She is described as wearing a Medici or fan collar (rather than a full neck ruff), a pearl necklace and a dress with bodice and full skirt, with raised details to illustrate embroidered geometric designs.

The style of clothing portrayed is designed to enforce social conditioning as clothing at this time was highly gendered and governed by strict laws and regulations to maintain these divisions, known as the Statutes of Apparel. The social position of individuals could be instantly recognised by their clothing, for example, wool, linen and sheepskin were restricted to the poorer classes. Some of the laws passed included one in 1536 that stipulated that poor children (aged between five and fourteen) who entered service were to be given a set of clothes, and in 1571 another one, aimed at supporting the English wool trade, required everyone (except royalty and nobility) aged six or older to wear a woollen cap on Sundays and holidays.

Tudor babies were usually completely and tightly swaddled and only unwrapped a few times a day as it was believed swaddling would help protect their bones. Younger children, both boys and girls, wore clothing similar to adult women's dress.

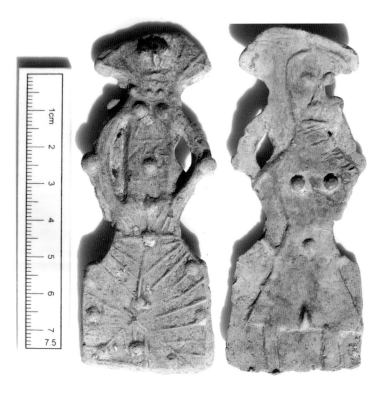

A cast-lead
toy doll of a
noble woman.
(NCL-DB1E00)

12. Gold posey ring (SF-E725DB)
Post-medieval (AD 1650–1800)
Found near Brockley, Suffolk. Width 5.2 mm, diameter 17.2 mm
Identified and recorded by Anna Booth.

The exchange of rings with an engraved motto on the inside of the band was common from the sixteenth to eighteenth centuries. The phrase inside this posey ring states 'I mourne with silence' indicating it may have been related to a bereavement, the small size suggesting it may have been worn by a child. Until relatively recently, death was a constant presence in the life of children, who regularly experienced the loss of siblings or parents. As such, until the later twentieth century, children were included in death and mourning rituals. To give some examples, the will of Sir David Owen (dated 1529) specified the wearing of gowns of black cloth by his children, while Hannah Bennett's will (dated 1730) included a bequest of mourning rings to numerous family members, including her grandchildren and great-grandchildren to wear in remembrance. A mourning bracelet for a child can be seen in the Museum of London collections online (object 28.88/1).

Gold posey finger ring decorated with floral pattern in relief and inscription on inside. (SF-E725DB)

Chapter 3
Education and Work

Children, except for those from more affluent families, have always contributed to household labour, which in and of itself is a form of learning. Physical evidence of children engaged in family or community endeavours can be seen at prehistoric sites where the wear patterns recorded on children's teeth are indicative of the repeated pulling and stretching of animal or plant material. Analysis of pottery from sites in eastern England has shown that children as young as five to seven years old were engaged in decorating pottery in the early to middle Bronze Age. By both Roman and medieval standards, once a child reached the age of seven they were expected to undertake more responsibility in

Post-medieval copper-alloy trade token. Halfpenny of James Ellis, grocer, of Cavendish (Suffolk), dated AD 1669. Fifteen poor children bound to apprenticeships attended a free school in Cavendish, of which James Ellis was a trustee. (ESS-C4BC97)

This small pot has been described as a possible 'practice' pot by an inexperienced potter, dated to AD 1000–1300. (NLM-55FC41)

the family. Education was the preserve of the wealthy. In medieval England one option for older children was to pursue an apprenticeship, which would last several years. Rather than learn a trade from a parent, the apprentice was placed with the tradesperson and instead of being paid they could expect board and clothing to be provided. The Industrial Revolution provided endless work for children, who were considerably cheaper to employ and easier to control than their adult counterparts. During the period of the Industrial Revolution there were few safeguarding rules and children endured horrific and abusive conditions. Compulsory education for those aged between five and ten years old did not come into force in England until the late nineteenth century.

13. Hand axe (NMS-71AF1F)
Palaeolithic (600,000–150,000 BC)
Found at Happisburgh, Norfolk. Length 54.5 mm, weight 39 g
Identified and recorded by Jason Gibbons.

This is one of several hand axes from Happisburgh that are notable for their small size (see also NMS-0D00D4,NMS-B9A3EC and NMS-F81FD1). Their exact function is unknown, although their size has been used to suggest the possibility that they were practice pieces for children. Flint knapping requires considerable skill, and it is likely children would have learnt this skill alongside adults. Detailed recording of flint working at other prehistoric sites has enabled the movements of individual flint knappers to be traced, and for different levels of experience to be seen in finished products. Hand axes are functional tools meant to be used, primarily in butchery, so it is more likely that in this case the small size is because it was meant to be used by children.

Happisburgh itself is famous for being the earliest known site of human activity in Britain when, in 2013, coastal erosion revealed human footprints thought to be more than 840,000 years old; the group of five individuals included adults and children.

Left and opposite: Small flint hand axe. (NMS-71AF1F)

28

29

14. Hornbook (LANCUM-5727FE)
Post-medieval (AD 1600–1700)
Found at Nateby, Cumbria. Length 53 mm, weight 15.82 g
Identified and recorded by Dot Boughton.

Hornbooks were used from the mid-fifteenth century as a means to teach children the alphabet. A page with either the alphabet or Lord's Prayer (sometimes both) written on either paper or vellum was covered with a thin sheet of horn, held in place by a wooden frame with a handle so it could be carried by a child. Small hornbooks, cast in metal, silver or, in the case of the PAS, examples in lead, could have been used for learning, although they may also have been played with as toys (see record SWYOR-26EE02). There are numerous metal examples listed on the PAS database, some with additional details including one with an image on the reverse of a woman in late sixteenth-century dress (SUR-23EAC4). The name of the maker is included on another (YORYM-FA8FF1) with the phrase 'Thomas of other good art made me. 1670'.

The handle of this lead-alloy hornbook is shaped like a doll's head, with possible further heads of dolls on the reverse. The obverse is decorated with the alphabet within a border frame. (LANCUM-5727FE)

A lead-alloy hornbook decorated on one side with a woman in sixteenth-century dress and the alphabet on the obverse, *c.* AD 1500–1700, length 52.6 mm. (SUR-23EAC4)

A lead-alloy hornbook with five lines of text stamped on the reverse reading: 'THOMAS// OFOTHER//DDEBO[-]//ESMEFIC//IT.(hatching)1670' ('Thomas of other good art made me. 1670'), length 44 mm. (YORYM-FA8FF1)

15. Child's thimble (IOW-C49EC9)
Post-medieval (AD 1650–1750)
Found on the Isle of Wight. Diameter 12.5 mm, weight 1.7 g
Identified and recorded by Lewis Ferrero.

From the mid-fourteenth century until the end of the seventeenth century metal thimbles in England were imported from mainland Europe. In the 1690s a Dutchman called John Lofting started making thimbles in London and went on to mass-produce thimbles including those for use by children. The example shown here is a Lofting Type III with its distinctive 'waffle' decoration, dated to the post-medieval period (AD 1650–1750). Children of all social classes would have had use for thimbles, as needlecraft was a key skill, particularly for girls. Embroidered samplers could be a personal reference of patterns, a demonstration of skill, and also used to teach basic literacy in preparing girls for a life in service.

Thimbles can be grouped into broad types, such as ring-type, domed and open-top forms, and although they can be made from various materials, only those of metal have been recorded by the PAS. Of over 5,000 thimbles on the database (not including palm-guards used by sailmakers and leatherworkers), at least sixty have been cited as possibly intended

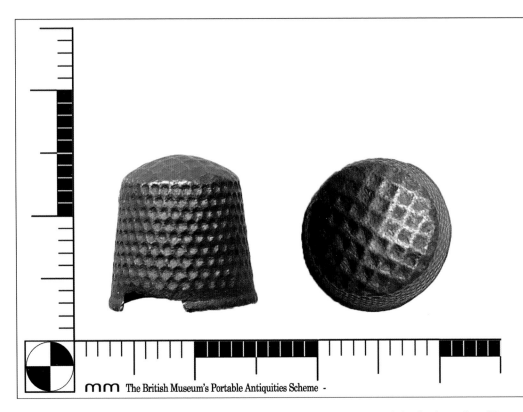

The British Museum's Portable Antiquities Scheme -

Copper-alloy domed thimble with circular machine-stamped pits around the body and waffle pattern on the top. (IOW-C49EC9)

Above left and above right: Silver thimble decorated on one side with a scrolled cartouche and the initials 'E B'. (GLO-48C9D7)

for use by children, although this figure may be higher. Thimbles for children are often recognised by having a small open diameter of less than 12mm, and at least two examples on the database have much smaller diameters of 7.5mm (SUSS-B18227; DUR-4D280D).

The vast majority of thimbles were manufactured in copper alloy, although some silver examples are listed, including two early eighteenth-century thimbles that feature the owner's initials (GLO-48C9D7; NMGW-4B4EDF).

16. Slate pencil (NLM-93C459)
Post-medieval-modern (AD 1880–1920)
Found at Winterton, North Lincolnshire. Length 32.8 mm, weight 1.77 g
Identified and recorded by Martin Foreman.

No modern school trip to recreate a Victorian school day is complete without using a slate pencil and board as these were a ubiquitous part of classroom equipment from the mid to late nineteenth century and into the twentieth century. The Education Act (1870) was the first legal response to increasing calls for free, non-religious, compulsory education at a national level. By 1880 all children aged five to ten were required to attend school, however many families could not afford the fees. In 1891 free education for this age group was achieved, and in 1893 this was extended to include children up to the age of eleven. Pencils containing graphite were first produced in England in the mid-sixteenth century, although it wasn't until the nineteenth century that they were mass-produced. Slate pencils and boards were, however, far more economical compared with pencil or ink and paper and were used for the younger children, while older children might use a nib with ink. The slate board could be wiped clean with a damp cloth (or clothing) to enable work to be started again, an act often related to the phrase 'to wipe the slate clean'.

Hexagonal section slate pencil. (NLM-93C459)

17. Workhouse medal (PUBLIC-ABD28A)
Post-medieval (AD 1785)
Found at Spilsby, Lincolnshire. Diameter 36 mm, weight 20.3 g
Identified and recorded by Kevin Woodward.

Images of workhouses are synonymous with Victorian Britain, although the origin of these institutions can be traced back to the fourteenth century. The church historically was the main provider of poor relief, although this support was interrupted following the Dissolution of the Monasteries by Henry VIII. Various laws were passed to try and reform provision until in the 1780s parishes were able to join to form unions and share costs. This copper-alloy medal is a rare survivor of an initiative across parishes in Lincolnshire in the 1780s and 1790s to encourage and reward children in learning and industry, only two of which on the PAS database have the child's name recorded. The text below comes from a description of the scheme by F. M. Eden writing in 1797 (more information on this is given on the PAS record for this object):

> ...teaching all poor children in the district to knit before they were six, and to spin before they were nine years of age. Towards the end of the year 1783, these laudable views were much assisted by the establishment of a Society, for the promotion of industry, by distributing premiums, in various articles of clothing, amongst such children, of certain ages and descriptions, within the district, as should, within a given time, produce the greatest quantity of work, of different kinds, and of the best quality.

A copper-alloy-plated medal issued by the Society of Industry, founded in 1783.
(PUBLIC-ABD28A)

The Poor Law Amendment Act of 1834 was designed to overhaul the system of poor relief. Although intended to provide accommodation and work for those in need of support, conditions in Victorian workhouses were harsh and particularly grim for children, as illustrated by Charles Dickens in *Oliver Twist*. Workhouse tokens such as that illustrated below were issued by some workhouses to be used by the poor with local shopkeepers.

A copper-alloy medal issued by the Society of Industry to a boy named Sam Wright, aged ten, between 1790 and 1799, diameter 36 mm. (LIN-16C4CD)

The British Museum's Portable Antiquities Scheme

Birmingham workhouse token, AD 1811, diameter 25 mm. (LEIC-DF2C4D)

18. Sunday school medallion (IOW-72AE51)
Post-medieval (AD 1880)
Found on the Isle of Wight. Diameter 45 mm, weight 24.55 g
Identified and recorded by Lewis Ferrero.

Established by Christian philanthropists in the late 1700s, these schools provided some basic education for working families. The earliest recorded schools opened in 1751 and 1769, however, 1780 is generally taken as the start date for the movement by one of its key figures, Robert Raikes. He is commemorated in this medallion, which reads:

Obverse: 'CENTENARY OF SUNDAY SCHOOL 1880 // ROBERT RAIKES'
Reverse: 'SUFFER THE LITTLE CHILDREN // TO COME UNTO ME'

Robert Raikes believed that education would deter working children from a life of crime, and much of the Sunday school syllabus focused on Christian teachings. Children in the late eighteenth and early nineteenth centuries endured harsh working conditions and extremely long hours. By the early nineteenth century their working day was restricted to 12 hours, although their working week included Saturdays, leaving Sunday as the only free day. Sunday schools were cross-denominational and were hugely popular by the mid-nineteenth century. Sunday schools encouraged learning and attendance by giving out prizes, principally books and certificates, like the one illustrated overleaf.

Copper-alloy medallion of Robert Raikes, 1880. (IOW-72AE51)

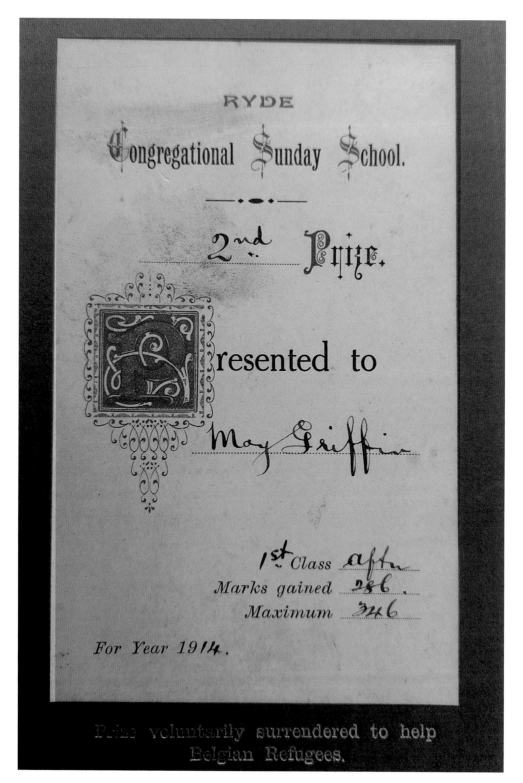

Sunday school certificate, awarded 1914. (Image author's collection)

Chapter 4
Toys

This section is, perhaps unsurprisingly, the best represented on the PAS database. A search on the database using the term 'Toy' brings up 2,163 records, of which 1,727 are of post-medieval date and 1,010 are of lead-alloy material, reflecting that many objects are metal detected finds. Geographical biases are also noticeable, with almost 300 'Toy' objects apiece recorded from NLM (North Lincolnshire) and LON (London), perhaps a reflection of the importance individual finders place on what are comparatively recent objects and

Oh! what good fun to wake one day,   And find the nursery Toys at play!

Postcard showing toys in the nursery, *c.* 1930. (Image author's collection)

the willingness of the FLO to record relatively modern items. A wide selection of objects fit into relatively narrow categories, including ceramic doll fragments, metal-alloy fragments of toy soldiers, farm animals and figurines. Household miniatures and doll's-house-related items are also well represented, as are objects relating to games of chance. Finds listed as 'Toy' have, therefore, been separated out into general toys, dolls and figurines, household miniature toys, and games. As more objects that fit the 'Toy' category are recorded, clearer patterns of childhood play can be explored; play is not limited to the home, and looking at where toys were lost may prove insightful in understanding the spaces children inhabited.

One of most famous images of children at play is that by Pieter Bruegel the Elder, painted in the sixteenth century. The painting features children engaged with toys and playing games, many examples of which are covered in this exploration of toys on the PAS and shows that the basics of play have not really changed that significantly. The painting is on display at the Kunsthistorisches Museum in Vienna but can be viewed on the museum webpage. In Britain, the word 'toy' itself did not come to be associated with a plaything rather than something that was just frivolous until the sixteenth century.

The introduction of the hollow-casting technique in the late nineteenth century revolutionised the production of lead toys, enabling them to be made more quickly and sold more cheaply. The materials and manufacture of toys have changed dramatically in the last 150 years, and combined with increases in family income and free time meant toy sales increased; today the UK toy industry is estimated to be worth over £4.7 billion to the economy, £1.4 billion of which is specifically aimed at toddlers and young children.

19. Toy sheep (NLM-18C0B2)
Modern (AD 1922–60)
Found at Market Rasen, East Midlands. Length 45.9 mm, weight 22.03 g
Identified and recorded by Martin Foreman.

Hollow-cast lead-alloy toys were first manufactured in the 1890s by Britains, a leading British toy company. Although initially focused on toy soldiers, they introduced the Farm Range in 1921 to counter reduced sales of military toys, which fell out of favour after the First World War. Initially the farm set comprised thirty pieces, with more added over subsequent years. Although this animal has no maker's stamp, others on the database can be assigned to Britains (for example NFLM-932BAA). Further examples of lead-alloy animals on the database are of similar date but either made at different scales to that used by Britains (who used 1:32) or made using different methods, for example, DENO-754624, which is at 1:32 but solid-cast rather than hollow-cast. In the mid-1950s Britains started making their farm toys in plastic and in 2021 celebrated a centenary of producing agricultural toys.

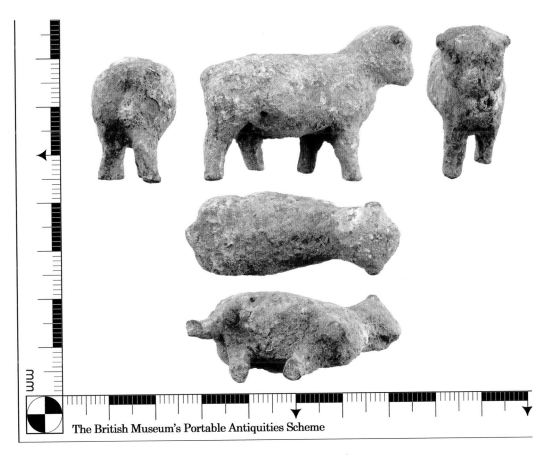

The British Museum's Portable Antiquities Scheme

Lead-alloy, hollow-cast toy sheep, scale 1:32. (NLM-18C0B2)

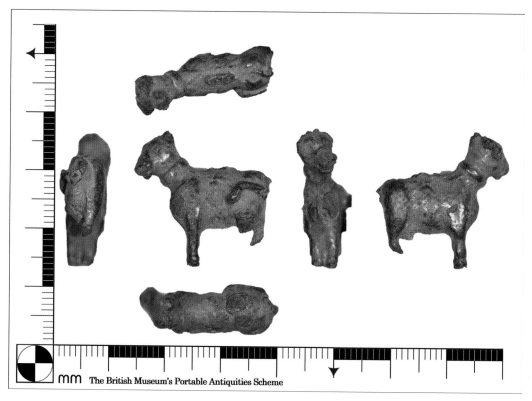

Lead-alloy, solid-cast toy animal, scale 1:32, *c.* AD 1920–60. (DENO-754624)

Lead-alloy, solid-cast toy pig, *c.* AD 1800–1900. (YORYM-230F64)

20. Meccano toy aeroplane (NLM-BC9BC5)
Modern (AD 1950–60)
Found in Walesby, Lincolnshire. Length 62.7 mm, weight 20.44 g
Identified and recorded by Martin Foreman.

One of the classic British toy makers, Meccano, appears on the PAS database. This example stamped 'DINKY TOYS/METEOR' and 'MADE IN ENGLAND BY MECCANO' is a good example of a lead-alloy twin-engine jet aeroplane. Identified by the finder as a Gloster Meteor, these planes were brought into service on 27 July 1944 as the only jet fighter used by the Allies during the Second World War. Despite its high crash rate, it remained an important element of air defence into the 1950s with 3,875 built.

A second example of a model plane, also from West Lindsey, is a model passenger plane again stamped Meccano and possibly 'Worth' as in Woolworth. The company chairman of Woolworths, William Stephenson, was seconded by the British government to oversee aircraft production during the Second World War, but he also recognised that toys had a key role in maintaining child morale both then and in the post-war period. Woolworths endeavoured to keep toy prices affordable during the war, at a cost of no more than sixpence, and as such became a much-loved shop to a generation of children. From the 1930s the demand for war-themed toys started to increase, although during the war years materials other than metal were used for toy manufacture and toys could be made from recycled objects, as might be the case with the copper-alloy Spitfire below (DEV-1EE409).

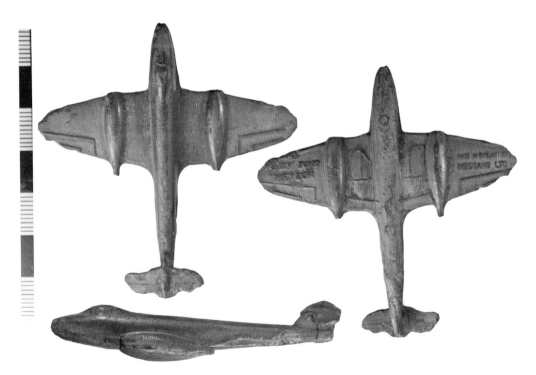

Lead-alloy toy Meteor plane, scale 1:200, *c.* AD 1950–60. (NLM-BC9BC5)

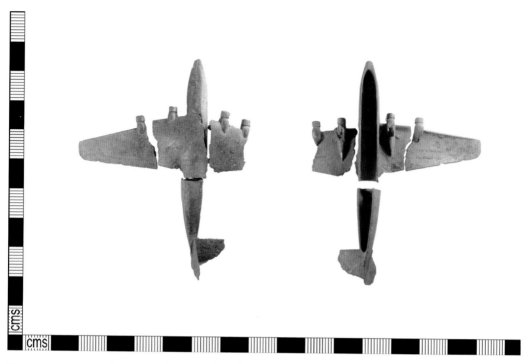

Toy passenger aeroplane, *c.* AD 1935–50, length 150 mm. (PUBLIC-2C41E9)

Toy aeroplane, possibly a Spitfire, *c.* AD 1935–45, length 27.1 mm. (DEV-1EE409)

21. Toy car (NLM-5C883F)
Modern (AD 1950–60)
Found at Blyton, Lincolnshire, in 2019. Length 50 mm, weight 17.29 g
Identified and recorded by Martin Foreman.

This toy car is stamped with the maker's name, Lesney. Another of the British toymakers, Lesney, was founded in 1947, although due to its distinctive packaging it became better known as Match Box Toys, and formally registered the name Matchbox in 1953. This car is one of the 1-75 series, famously scaled down to fit in the 'matchbox' branding. It is a model of an MG T-series, the TD midget, produced between 1950 and 1953. Matchbox toy cars were highly accurate die-cast miniatures, the details and affordable price ensuring their popularity. They maintained dominance in the small toy-car market regardless of the other popular British brands of the time, Dinky and Corgi. Despite the purchase of the Matchbox brand by competitors in the 1980s, the name Matchbox has remained synonymous with small toy-car manufacture.

Zinc-alloy toy
car, *c.* 1965.
(NLM-5C883F)

Matchbox No. 38a, 1-75 series Bantam Karrier refuse collector, first manufactured in 1957. (Image author's collection)

22. Figural cap bomb (DUR-C93449)
Post-medieval (AD 1820–1925)
Found at Shincliffe, County Durham. Length 31.48 mm, weight 34.9 g
Identified and recorded by Des Murphy.

Children love things that go bang, and these novelty heads certainly did that! They were designed for a small fulminate charge to be inserted into the mouth so when the object was thrown against a hard surface the jaw would close, detonating the charge and resulting in a loud bang. The force of the explosion often caused the jaw to fall out, which might explain why this is the only example on the database to still be intact. These figural cap bangs were popular from the mid- to late 1800s and often represented famous people of the time. Into the late 1950s with the advent of the 'race for space', cap bombs increasingly took the form of rockets and manufacture changed from metal to plastic (there are some examples of metal versions on the database such as NLM-EA3B97).

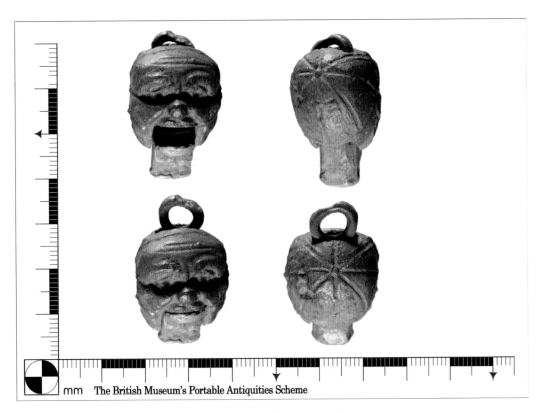

Complete lead toy head for percussive caps. (DUR-C93449)

23. Child's rattle (SUR-D1D57A)
Post-medieval (AD 1800–1900)
Found at Palace Riverside, Greater London. Length 30 mm, weight 6.22 g
Identified and recorded by Simon Maslin.

Rattles can serve many functions, for example, spiritual or musical, but here we are looking at those made specifically for children. We have references to rattles being used to distract or entertain babies from Greek and Roman authors and later, for example, an early sixteenth-century Latin textbook which includes the line 'I will buy a rattle to still my crying baby'. The rattle illustrated below is made of silver and would have held a piece of coral to aid teething, although wolf teeth could also be used, and an example of this type from London has been dated to the 1540s. By the nineteenth and twentieth centuries ivory and mother of pearl were replacing coral as a material for teething in this form of rattle. A complete post-medieval bone rattle from London, probably made in India and of a type common in the nineteenth century, is a good example of a rattle made in a material other than metal.

mm   The British Museum's Portable Antiquities Scheme

Silver rattle.
(SUR-D1D57A)

48

Post-medieval bone rattle. (© Andy Chopping/MOLA)

Mrs Jacob Hurd and Child, William Johnston, *c.* AD 1762. (Image courtesy of Metropolitan Museum of Art. Public Domain)

24. Pair of whirligigs (SWYOR-1188D8)
Post-medieval (AD 1600–1800)
Found at Clapham cum Newby, North Yorkshire. Wheel 1: diameter 55.1 mm,
weight 37.11 g; Wheel 2: length 46.27 mm, weight 15.92 g
Identified and recorded by Chris Scriven.

Also known as buzzers, buzz wheels or twirly whirlys, these toys are spinning objects with one or more parts. Threaded onto a string or cord, the tensioning and release of the cord causes the whirligig to spin, the serrated edges creating the characteristic whirring sound.

Spinning objects have a long-held fascination for children and adults alike, with many examples of different types of spinning toys recorded from the prehistoric period through to modern times. Whirligigs of the type shown here were popular throughout the post-medieval period, and those on the database occur in lead or other metal alloys.

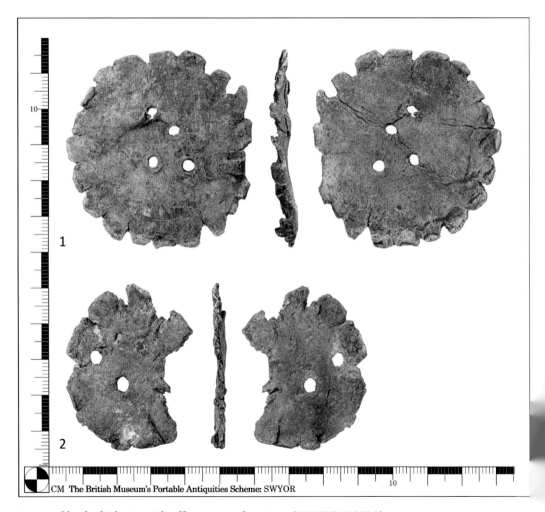

CM The British Museum's Portable Antiquities Scheme: SWYOR

A pair of lead whirligigs with off-centre perforations. (SWYOR-1188D8)

Token re-used as a whirligig, *c.* AD 1600–1800, diameter 34.6 mm. (IOW-A3C45E)

Often, they appear crudely made, invariably cut down from other objects. One from the Isle of Wight, for example, has the initials B W H and has been identified as a possible token that has been re-used (IOW-A3C45E). A typology of whirligigs from London includes a number from re-used coins, tokens and even a toy frying pan. Whirligigs were also popular at this time in North America, with examples from Jamestown, USA, and other early sites, of whirligigs made from hammered out lead musket balls. One example on the database of lead shot that has been flattened shows how suitable these were for adaptation (NLM-258335). Their recovery as surface finds and their history as re-used objects does not help in dating them more precisely, however, one example recovered from an archaeologically secure context in Britain (AD 1675–1700), combined with their occurrence on colonial sites, does indicate a peak popularity in the eighteenth century.

25. Wooden whipping top (SUR-C7C19E)
Post-medieval (AD 1800–1900)
Found at Nutfield, Surrey. Length 63.1 mm, weight 33.8 g
Identified and recorded by Simon Maslin.

As we have seen with whirligigs, making things spin seems to have always held appeal for children, and spinning tops are one of the oldest toys found by archaeologists. A spinning top was even found in the tomb of King Tutankhamun, placed over 3,000 years ago. With all spinning tops the aim is to keep the momentum going and the different ways of achieving this are shown in the variety of types, for example, throwing tops, pump tops, twirling tops and whip tops. The whipping top illustrated here is made of wood and is pear-shaped with an iron point. It would have been set in motion and kept spinning by use of a string whip, and these toys were very popular in the Victorian period. Four letters, AH and HV, have been written on the top in black ink, probably by the owner.

This toy was found with a child's shoe (SUR-C78410), approximately a modern child's size 10 for a child aged about five. Both had been hidden in the wall of a sixteenth-century building.

Wooden spinning top.
(SUR-C7C19E)

26. Whistle (PUBLIC-B5590B)
Post-medieval (AD 1850–1900)
Found at Folkton, North Yorkshire. Diameter 26.6 mm, weight 11.7 g
Identified and recorded by Stephen Auker.

Whistles on the database include several that were designed for use by children, including this metal example imitating a clay smoking pipe. When complete the whistle would have had a long stem with a narrow bore hole and the bowl would have been covered by a lid with a central small hole. As air was blown down the stem, the lid covering would have prevented most of the air leaving the bowl and created a piercing whistle sound as the air was forced through the lid hole. Recent research has shown these are likely to have been mass-produced in Germany, which at the time exported large numbers of metal toys to England. Toys and confectionery modelled on smoking continued into the later twentieth century, although following changes in social attitudes towards smoking such toys and sweets fell out of fashion.

Other whistles for children include a lead-alloy bird (NLM-855A13), some versions of which would have held water and when blown would make an amusing warbling sound. Whistles to entertain babies and infants also provided a teething element such as a piece of coral, similar to some contemporary rattles. A good example of this type on the database is WILT-6D1427, which can be paralleled with a whistle teether from Jamestown, USA, dated to the start of the seventeenth century.

A cast lead-alloy whistle in the form of a pipe bowl. (PUBLIC-B5590B)

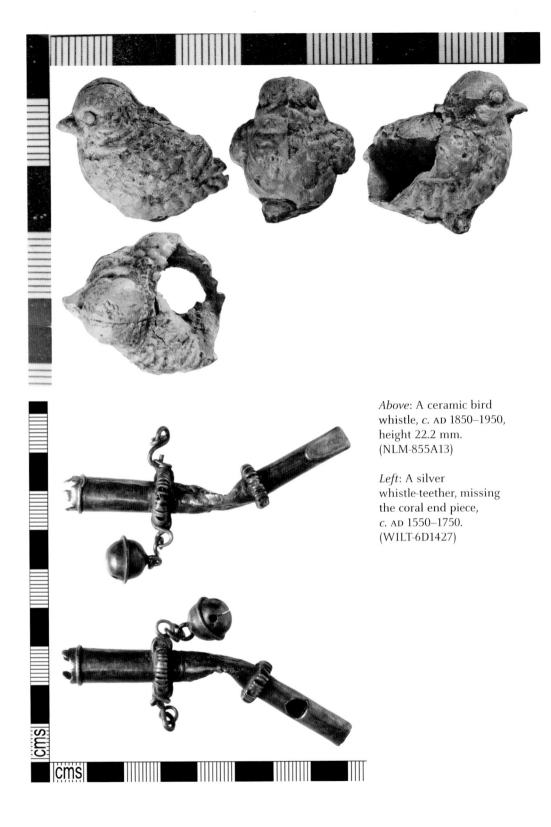

Above: A ceramic bird whistle, *c.* AD 1850–1950, height 22.2 mm. (NLM-855A13)

Left: A silver whistle-teether, missing the coral end piece, *c.* AD 1550–1750. (WILT-6D1427)

27. Toy gun (SF-F30CAA)
Post-medieval (AD 1600–50)
Found at Forest Heath, Suffolk. Length 92.6 mm, weight 29.40 g
Identified and recorded by Phil Hughes.

This cast copper-alloy toy gun is a musket-type, hollow-cast and with the distinctive fishtail butt that also featured on full-size muskets in the early seventeenth century. It is decorated with a punched ring-and-dot design to imitate the decorative inlays incorporated in the original models. During the seventeenth century, model firearms were mass-produced for the amusement of adults and children and were designed to be fired, not dissimilar to the popular cap-guns of the nineteenth and twentieth centuries (WREX-ED803A). Most toy guns on the database fall within this musket category, and one example is unusual in that it was found with the ramrod (SOM-40C211).

Above: Copper-alloy toy musket. (SF-F30CAA)

Right: Incomplete modern lead toy cap gun in the form of a flintlock pistol, *c.* AD 1800–1900, length 91.8 mm. (WREX-ED803A)

28. Toy cannon (DOR-B44194)
Post-medieval (AD 1700–1800)
Found at Ringwood, Hampshire. Length 104.67 mm, weight 42.54 g
Identified and recorded by Ciorstaidh Hayward Trevarthen.

This object is a copper-alloy cast toy cannon dated stylistically from the early eighteenth to nineteenth centuries. These toys were modelled on the cannon in use on warships and fortifications of the day which from the late sixteenth century were being mass-produced. There are almost 400 currently recorded on the database and they are possibly the most

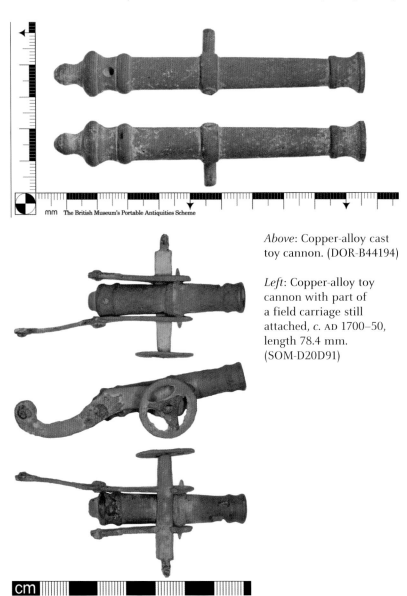

Above: Copper-alloy cast toy cannon. (DOR-B44194)

Left: Copper-alloy toy cannon with part of a field carriage still attached, *c.* AD 1700–50, length 78.4 mm. (SOM-D20D91)

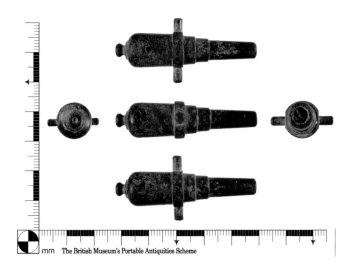

Copper-alloy toy cannon,
c. AD 1750–1900, length
51.4 mm. (HAMP-567512)

mm   The British Museum's Portable Antiquities Scheme

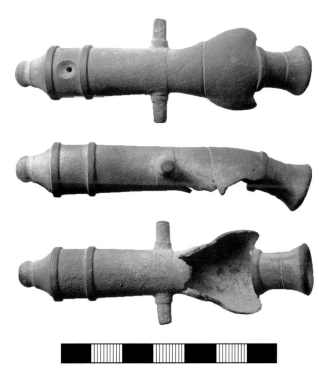

Toy cannon with evidence
of accidental mis-firing,
c. AD 1700–1800, length
92.97 mm. (SUR-F6DB32)

frequently found toys of this date outside of London. One example (SOM-D20D91) is unusual in still having part of the field carriage attached. Perhaps alarmingly by modern health and safety standards, these cannons were mostly designed to be fired – children at the time would have had easy access to the gunpowder required to set the charge and to an assortment of materials suitable to use as shot. The cannon would have been set in a carriage, and the larger cannons would have had an impressive range. Occasionally the cannon misfired, as was probably the case for this one found in Surrey (SUR-F6DB32) where the force of the explosion has torn the underside between the trunnions and the raised band.

Chapter 5
Dolls, Soldiers and Figurines

The oldest dolls recorded by the PAS are of lead, although later ceramic dolls are also represented. There are no examples in wood, bone, cloth, *papier mâché*, wax or plastic. For most of their history, dolls have been representations of adult women, and were dressed according to the adult fashions of the time. A Roman doll found in Britain can be seen at Reading Museum (online catalogue) and part of another Roman doll was found (and is on display) at Corbridge on Hadrian's Wall. Dolls imitating babies are a relatively modern phenomenon, first appearing in the mid-nineteenth century, although it was not until the 1930s that baby dolls became more interactive by drinking and wetting their nappy. Fashion dolls had a huge revival in 1959 with the launch of Barbie, followed by Sindy in 1963 and Action Man in 1966.

Alongside dolls, toy soldiers are well represented on the PAS, with an array of flat figures and both solid and hollow-cast examples. Although most are incomplete, some retain traces of original paintwork.

Lead figurine of a woman in long flowing garment with waist belt, thought to be a child's toy, possibly home-made, AD 1200–1500, height 82.2 mm. (NLM-15409A)

29. Lead figure (DUR-2F2D86)
Post-medieval (AD 1600–1700)
Found at Loftus, Redcar and Cleveland. Length 58.32 mm, weight 18.9 g
Identified and recorded by Frances McIntosh.

There are a number of figurines dating from the sixteenth to eighteenth centuries on the database comprising flat, lead cast, male and female representations. This male figure is unusual in that he is not obviously a military person, lacking any weaponry, whereas soldier 'flats' were common in the seventeenth century, for example SOM-CA72E2. The PAS record describes him thus, 'He is wearing a hat and has shoulder length hair. He has four large circular buttons down his coat and some decoration on his ruff and the edges of his coat.'

Female figures include the complete example discussed in Chapter 2 (NCL-DB1E00) and various other partial objects such as the lead female figure below (LVPL-F001D5).

Cast lead-alloy flat figurine
of horse and rider.
(DUR-2F2D86)

Above left: Incomplete lead-alloy toy doll, *c.* AD 1550–1650, length 62.14 mm. (LVPL-F001D5)

Above right: Incomplete lead-alloy cast male figurines in military dress with baggy breeches, a fitted, sleeveless jerkin or waistcoat over a jacket and traces of a high neck ruff, *c.* AD 1600–1750. (SOM-CA72E2)

30. Frozen Charlotte (PUBLIC-6EDC24)
Post-medieval (AD 1800–1900)
Found at Cottingham, East Riding of Yorkshire. Height 35.7 mm, weight 6.2 g
Identified and recorded by a member of the public.

A doll with a rather morbid background was very popular in Britain and North America from the 1850s until the 1920s. Also known as Bathing Dolls, China Babies and Penny Dolls, there is some debate as to when these dolls were first referred to as Frozen Charlottes. They did, however, become incredibly popular following the publication of a poem in 1843 entitled 'A Corpse Going to a Ball' originally penned by Elizabeth Oakes Smith. The poem recounts the rather tragic tale of a young girl who refuses to cover up her fine dress to keep warm on her way to a ball and is then found frozen to death by the time her carriage arrives. A popular folk song at the time based on the poem also increased the interest in these dolls.

The dolls are moulded in one piece, in either porcelain or 'bisque', which is an unglazed porcelain. Produced in great numbers in Germany, these were originally bathing dolls (some have a hole on the back to drain water) but their arrival coincided with the tale

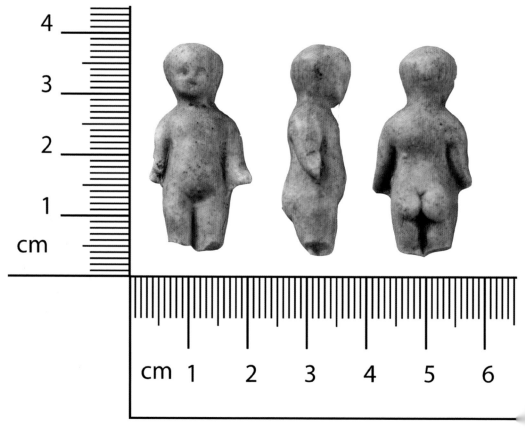

Frozen Charlotte figurine. (PUBLIC-6EDC24)

Set of incomplete Frozen Charlottes showing a range of sizes from 30 mm to 105 mm in height. (Image author's collection)

of poor Charlotte and their popularity grew. Some are glazed with colour, and the male version is known as a Frozen Charlie, after the beau that accompanied her on that fateful evening.

To date there are six possible examples on the PAS database, of which this is the most complete; however, various other examples can be seen in museum collections. Some of the PAS examples are in a red clay, rather than the traditional porcelain or bisque, one of which (NLM-0AC196) has been cited as an example of craftspeople in a traditional brick-and-tile-producing area making their own versions of these dolls for local children.

31. China doll head (NLM-42A225)
Post-medieval (AD 1775–1875)
Found at Brodsworth, Doncaster. Height 25.5 mm, weight 4.92 g
Identified and recorded by Martin Foreman.

Whereas Frozen Charlotte dolls were moulded as a one piece, the database also contains many other doll body parts that would have been attached to cloth bodies. This doll's head, probably manufactured in Germany, is one such example, and would have been part of a small doll, possibly for use in a doll's house. As a small doll, all her facial features are moulded and painted, whereas larger dolls could have inset eyes and eyelashes and hair attached rather than painted. Most dolls of this size were modelled at 1:12 scale (where 1 foot is represented by 1 inch), although she might be at 1:10, a scale more common in Germany. By way of a size comparison, modern fashion dolls such as Barbie are at a scale of 1:6 and Playmobil at 1:24.

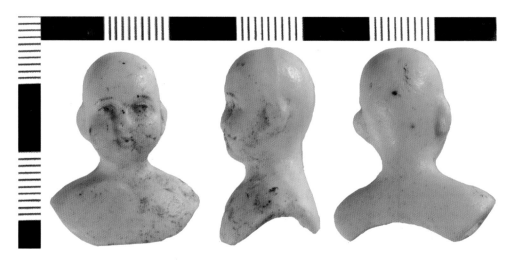

Above: Small ceramic doll's head. (NLM-42A225)

Left: Doll with ceramic head and limbs, cloth body. (Image author's collection)

32. Napoleon figurine (WMID-509CD9)
Post-medieval (AD 1803–93)
Found at Wyre Forest, Worcestershire. Height 33.1 mm, weight 12.3 g
Identified and recorded by Teresa Gilmore.

Soldiers have always been a popular subject for toy makers and here we have a cast lead-alloy figure of Napoleon I, Emperor of France (1804–15), one of several on the database.

Fear of a French invasion was very real for the people of Britain in the early eighteenth century, the Napoleonic Wars involving almost every European state. This fear mildly abated following British success at the Battle of Trafalgar (1805) but was not completely removed for another decade until Napoleon's defeat at the Battle of Waterloo (1815).

Toy soldiers were first mass-produced at the end of the eighteenth century, although they were prohibitively expensive for all but the most wealthy; in 1812 Napoleon himself ordered a 240-piece set of toy soldiers for his young son. In 1893 the British toy manufacturer Britains started producing toy soldiers in lead using the hollow-casting method which revolutionised the process.

Incomplete lead-alloy toy solider depicting Napoleon with arms crossed over chest. (WMID-509CD9)

33. Toy mounted soldier (ASHM-7B1559)
Post-medieval–modern (AD 1840–1960)
Found at Childrey, Oxfordshire. Height 28 mm, weight 10.4 g
Identified and recorded by Alison Pollard.

Most of the mounted soldiers recorded on the PAS database are incomplete, but this one is better preserved than most as it retains all but the horse's lower legs and still has traces of red paint intact. A cavalryman, these types of toys were mass-produced in the late nineteenth and twentieth centuries, including by the British toy company Britains, who pioneered the hollow-cast process. A large number of soldiers on the database have all been recorded in Lincolnshire, and a good example is NLM-A1C406, a British officer, as indicated by his sword. Solid-cast in lead in semi-flat form, this has been identified as of probable Continental manufacture.

The first half of the twentieth century saw toy soldiers produced in either lead or 'composition' (a mix of glue and sawdust). The ban on lead toys in 1966 saw companies focus entirely on the production of plastic soldiers, which had been gaining in popularity throughout the 1950s.

Lead-alloy figurine of calvary rider on a horse, *c.* AD 1840–1960. (ASHM-7B1559)

Lead-alloy solid-cast toy soldier of a British officer in overseas uniform, *c.* AD 1900–14, scale *c.* 1:40, height 45 mm. (NLM-A1C406)

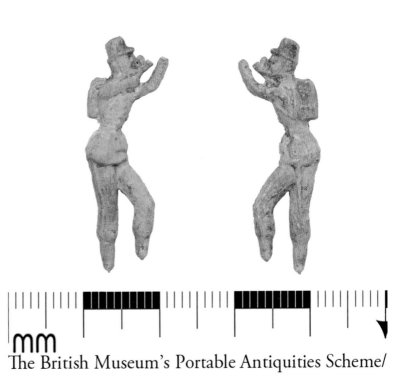

Incomplete lead-alloy toy infantryman solider, *c.* AD 1800–1900. (DEV-917E7B)

The British Museum's Portable Antiquities Scheme/

34. Classical figurine (WILT-7586D2)
Post-medieval (AD 1700–1900)
Found at Wherwell, Hampshire. Length 31 mm, weight 12.31 g
Identified and recorded by Jane Hanbridge.

This incomplete lead-alloy figurine is possibly a Greek or Roman soldier or official, described on the record as wearing breast and back armour, with a long skirt covering the upper legs. The angle of the arms, where broken, suggests they may have been outstretched which may indicate a charioteer. The bird imagery on the breastplate could be an eagle, which to the Romans represented power, strength and immortality, and featured on Roman army standards. The date of this figurine is uncertain. However, classical subjects (for example, Latin and ancient history) were key elements of education for boys from wealthy families in the eighteenth century. Another object that shows the influence of the classics in play is a small model Roman gladius sword in its scabbard (SWYOR-353071). The record for this sword states that, although Roman votive miniature swords have also been recorded, this example displays differences in the handle form which combined with the casting and overall condition is more in keeping with a later, post-medieval date.

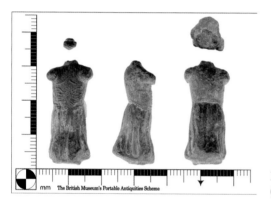

Incomplete lead-alloy figurine.
(WILT-7586D2)

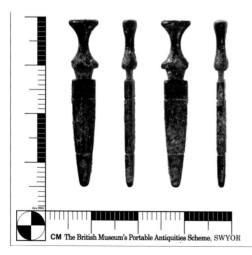

Miniature gladius sword, c. AD 1800–1950.
(SWYOR-353071)

Chapter 6
Miniature Household Toys

Most miniature household items date from the sixteenth century, increasing throughout the seventeenth and eighteenth centuries, although earlier examples and contemporary portrayals of children at play show that such objects have a longer history. Medieval cooking vessels, such as cauldrons and tableware, appear in miniature form as early as the thirteenth century, and small lead jugs imitated the full ceramic versions that would have been commonplace in homes. Toys imitating domestic life can be seen particularly clearly into the sixteenth century, as the repertoire of kitchen and table miniatures expanded to mirror domestic settings.

In the sixteenth and seventeenth centuries 'cabinet houses' were popular with wealthy women on the Continent to both display status and to educate young servants in household management. By the late eighteenth century doll's houses as we recognise them today

Doll's-house interior. (Image author's collection, courtesy of Carisbrooke Castle Museum)

0   Cm   1

Doll's-house window,
length 26.5 mm.
(NMGW-15F4F9)

Toy candlestick,
c. AD 1700–1800, height
74.6 mm. (LON-FF6C72)

really came into fashion and were a staple toy in the Victorian nursery, retaining their popularity ever since. A leading doll's-house maker in Britain was G. & J. Lines, which started production in the 1890s. Older doll's houses were not made to a standard scale, although this was remedied in the twentieth century as a scale of 1:18 was introduced for doll's houses. One of the most famous and elaborate doll's houses was created for Queen Mary in the 1920s by Sir Edwin Lutyens, and is still on display at Windsor Castle. All the big brand names of the day contributed miniatures to equip the house, which also has electricity and running water.

Above: Toy flat iron, *c.* AD 1840–1940, length 35 mm. (LANCUM-DCD6AA)

Right: Metal-alloy flat animal-skin rug with head and tail attached, *c.* AD 1700–1950, length 62 mm. (BUC-30E542)

There are numerous miniatures of objects used for food preparation and consumption recorded by the PAS, less so household objects such as furniture and domestic accessories, which tend to be found in larger collections such as those from London. This may be down to poor survival of these objects, but they are generally less common finds outside of sizeable urban centres.

35. Toy gridiron with fish (FAHG-C743A5)
Post-medieval (AD 1850–1900)
Found at Woolpit, Suffolk. Length 65.5 mm long, weight 4.2 g
Identified and recorded by Helen Geake.

A gridiron is a piece of cooking equipment used from the medieval period for toasting, grilling and broiling foodstuffs. This complete miniature lead-alloy example has a flat fish laid across a six-bar frame. A seventeenth- to eighteenth-century date is usually attributed to such gridirons, although this example was uncovered beneath the floorboards of a house built towards the end of the nineteenth century. It was found with a collection of other objects including slate pencils and a ceramic marble, possibly stashed away for safekeeping by a younger inhabitant.

Other toy items relating to food preparation that occur frequently on the database are dripping pans, the full-size versions being placed under meat cooking on a spit to collect the dripping hot fat. This example from Kent has very similar decoration to another toy dripping pan found in London.

Possibly the most ubiquitous cooking utensil in history is the cauldron, the oldest known examples in Britain dating from the Bronze Age. A cauldron is a cooking vessel that can be suspended over a fire by chains or supported in the centre of a fire by metal legs, as in this miniature example. A good comparison for this object occurs as an illustration in a medieval manuscript dating to the late thirteenth to early fourteenth centuries.

Lead-alloy
gridiron with fish.
(FAHG-C743A5)

The British Museum's Portable Antiquities Scheme

Above: Complete toy dripping pan, *c.* AD 1600–1750, height 36.75 mm. (KENT-EF33CC)

Right: Miniature cauldron, *c.* AD 1200–1500, height 41 mm. A parallel can be seen illustrated in the margins of a late thirteenth- to early fourteenth-century manuscript (British Library Royal MS 10 E IV, f. 108r.). (LEIC-8D2517)

71

36. Miniature lead-alloy jug (DUR-B35614)
Medieval (AD 1150–1450)
Found at Ryedale, North Yorkshire. Length 44.77 mm, weight 36.2 g
Identified and recorded by Ellie Cox.

Miniature lead toy jugs can be dated through comparison with their full-size pottery counterparts, many of which have been excavated from well-dated archaeological contexts. Jugs would have been common in medieval households, used primarily to hold wine, ale or beer, so their creation in miniature form is perhaps unsurprising. The jug shown here (DUR-B356140) is a copy of a baluster jug, a type common from the thirteenth to late fourteenth centuries. Miniature jugs also copied those made in metal, as in the case of object BH-128184, which is slightly later in date and might have been produced in the Netherlands. A complete stone mould used in the production of these miniatures is discussed in Chapter 8.

Miniature lead-alloy baluster jug. (DUR-B35614)

Right: Minature
lead-alloy baluster
jug, *c.* AD 1150–1300,
height 33 mm.
(GLO-C83C98)

Below: Miniature
copper-alloy baluster
jug, fifteenth century,
probably from
the Netherlands,
height 197.1 mm.
(BH-128184)

37. Miniature glass goblet (BH-1F0F22)
Post-medieval (AD 1500–1700)
Found at Berkhamsted, Hertfordshire. Height 22.4 mm, weight 7.7 g
Identified and recorded by Julian Watters.

Glass objects are relatively rare on the database, and especially so when looking at miniature toys of this type. This goblet is probably of a sixteenth- or seventeenth-century date and would have originally been green in colour. A miniature wine bottle within the Museum of London collection is also rare, if not unique in England. Drinking vessels in the form of metal cups are far more common, and also include some unusual forms, such as 'flat cups' (LON-661B25), the full-size type usually having been made in silver.

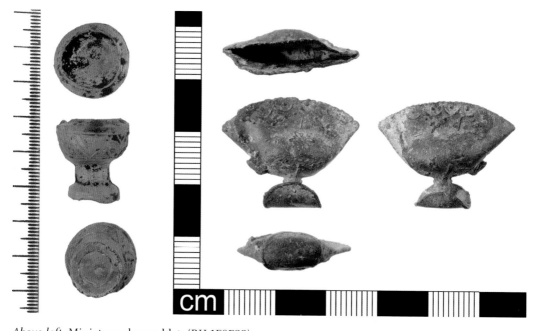

Above left: Miniature glass goblet. (BH-1F0F22)

Above right: Cast lead-alloy miniature standing bowl or flat cup, *c.* AD 1550–1600, height 20.42 mm. (LON-661B25)

38. Toy plate (WILT-88CCF8)
Post-medieval (AD 1650–1750)
Found in Heytesbury, Wiltshire. Diameter 48.2 mm, weight 33.29 g
Identified and recorded by Jane Hanbridge.

This circular, miniature lead dinner plate has a scalloped rim, decorated with raised pellets. Many of these miniature dinner plates were copies of ceramic versions, which by the mid-seventeenth century were often highly decorated. Whereas miniature jugs can be compared to their full-size ceramic counterparts as an aid for dating, this is less clear for dinner plates where there is seemingly little consistency in terms of size and decoration. They are most commonly circular in shape, although some more unusual octagonal shapes have also been recorded, such as LON-88601A.

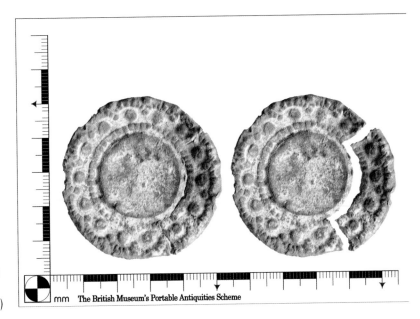

Miniature lead dinner plate. (WILT-88CCF8)

Miniature octagonal lead dinner plate, c. AD 1700–50, diameter 35 mm. (LON-88601A)

39. Toy chair (PUBLIC-7EFCE6)
Post-medieval (AD 1755–77)
Found at St Katherine's and Wapping, Tower Hamlets, London.
Height 78.56 mm, weight 17.21 g
Identified and recorded by a member of the public.

There are not many examples of toy furniture recorded on the database, but this is a good example, missing its legs, but otherwise complete. The style of the chair is comparable to the Ribband back chairs produced by Thomas Chippendale in the mid-eighteenth century. The seat of the chair is decorated, probably intended to represent a cushion. Other furniture pieces recorded by the PAS include three partial doors, possibly from buffets or cupboards.

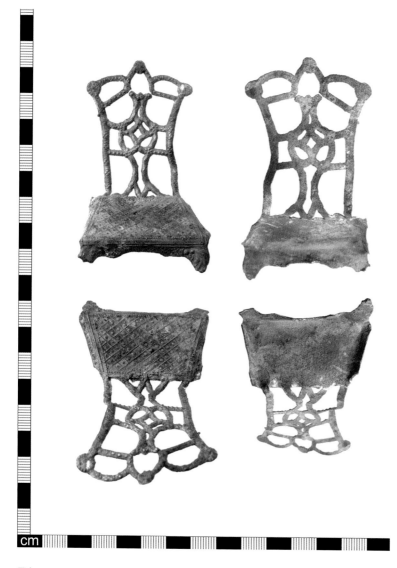

Miniature lead-alloy toy chair back and seat, legs missing. (PUBLIC-7EFCE6)

40. Toy fire shovel (LANCUM-9A592A)
Post-medieval (AD 1600–1800)
Found in Whalley, Lancashire. Length 127 mm, weight 32.27 g
Identified and recorded by Stuart Noon.

Of all the toy household items found, fire shovels are one of the most common, although complete examples, as here, are relatively rare. Fireside accessories including the likes of shovels, tongs, pokers, grates, scuttles and fireguards would have been commonplace in many homes by the post-medieval period, and all replicated in miniature. Beatrix Potter's *Tale of Two Bad Mice* features two naughty mice in a doll's house and the illustrations show many of the objects discussed here, including a novel use for a fire shovel.

Above left: Lead-alloy toy fire shovel. (LANCUM-9A592A)

Above right: Copper-alloy toy fire shovel, engraved with a diamond lattice design with a punched dot in the centre of each lozenge, *c*. AD 1600–1800. (NMS-2AF887)

Chapter 7
Games of Chance

A general distinction has been made here between toys (as specific objects) and games (a form of activity), although it is recognised that toys can also be used to play a game! When looking at board games, although individual game pieces might survive, they are by their nature less likely to figure on the PAS database. Other games, such as cards or puzzles, are likewise absent from the database. Some of the more well-known historical board games include the Royal Game of Ur, chess, backgammon, dominos, senet and mah-jong, whereas modern audiences may list Monopoly, Cluedo and Risk. Not all board games are aimed at children, although the many Roman examples of games involving a 'board' and pieces or counters in Britain shows that while it may have been a pastime for soldiers, many others in society could also have played. Games of chance involving a die or knucklebones have always been popular.

Above left: Lead-alloy domino piece, *c.* AD 1700–1900, length 30.8 mm. (WREX-A83904)

Above right: Monopoly boot gaming piece, *c.* AD 1935–2000, length 20.4 mm. (HAMP-E8C30F)

A Roman stone die, with values marked by a ring-and-dot design, *c.* AD 50–410, 8.33 mm x 8.11 mm. (LON-6181C7)

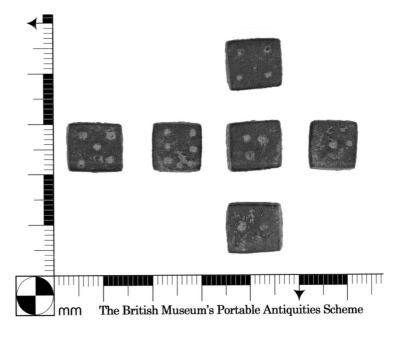

A complete copper-alloy die, with the values marked by drilled pits on each face, *c.* AD 1200–1800, 10.25 mm x 11.71 mm x 10.33 mm. Unlike modern dice, the faces do not all add up to 7. (YORYM-04DFEA)

41. Chess piece (LIN-BC6858)
Medieval (AD 1000–1400)
Found at Beckingham, Lincolnshire. Length 32 mm
Identified and recorded by Adam Daubney.

This chess piece is an early example of a King or Queen and probably made of carved bone. It can be dated by comparison to other examples recovered from archaeological contexts that range from the eleventh to fourteenth centuries. Another early example is the decorated King piece from London (LON-55F862), similarly dated (AD 1150–1350), although later pieces have also been recorded on the database including a post-medieval copper-alloy King piece (WMID-4D3688) and two pieces, a Queen and Bishop, possibly re-purposed as talismans and hidden in the wall of a building (LIN-F5A23A and LIN-F63D03).

Chess is a game learnt by many young people today for fun and to develop strategic thinking and problem-solving skills. However, in the past the allegory and symbolism within the game was also a way to re-enforce expected roles in society through the relationships between the different pieces. As a game it has a long history, possibly evolving from Chaturanga, a strategy game in India, which then spread through its popularity, reaching Western Europe in the eleventh century AD. The most well-known historical chess set in the UK was found on the Isle of Lewis, Scotland, in 1831. The Lewis Chessmen, as they are known, are elaborately carved examples made in Norway between AD 1150 and 1200 (Lewis was part of the Kingdom of Norway until 1266).

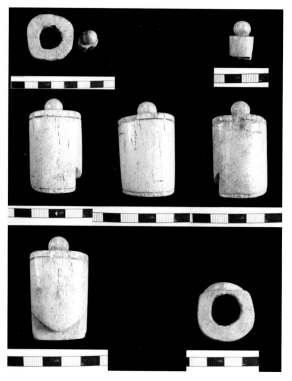

Bone chess piece. (LIN-BC6858)

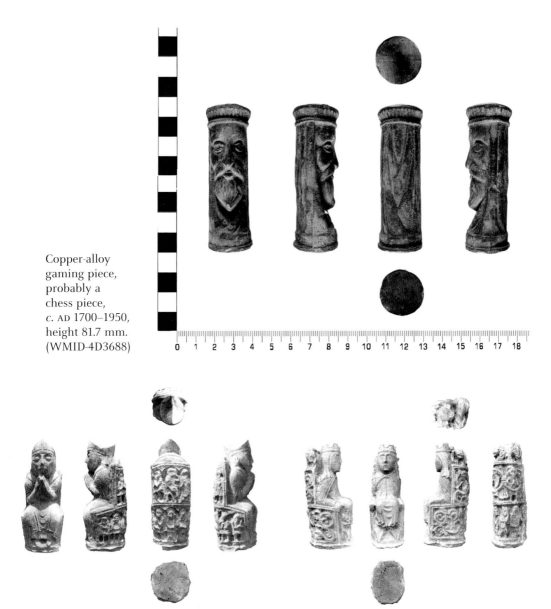

Copper-alloy gaming piece, probably a chess piece, c. AD 1700–1950, height 81.7 mm. (WMID-4D3688)

Above left: Both this piece and the one next to it (LIN-F5A23A) are made of plaster of Paris, and thought to be copies of a fourteenth-century German chess set form Leipzig, c. AD 1850–1950, height 65 mm. (LIN-F63D03)

Above right: Height 70 mm. (LIN-F5A23A)

Initially the preserve of the wealthy and monastic orders, chess sets are recorded in the wardrobe accounts of King Edward I (AD 1299–1300). Following the publication in 1474 of a book on chess by William Caxton, the game became more popular, particularly among children as it was seen as an educational tool. Increasingly, people from all social classes enjoyed playing chess.

42. Knucklebone (NLM-76C011)
Roman (AD 43–420)
Found at Roxby-cum-Risby, North Lincolnshire, in 2016. Length 19.1 mm, weight 11.19 g
Identified and recorded by Martin Foreman.

Roman pottery was often repaired using lead to 'plug' or fix the break between two pieces. However, the relative length and small size of the ends here makes this interpretation unlikely, and it is more probably a piece from a game known as knucklebones, like the modern game of jacks.

The basis of both these games revolves around throwing several objects into the air and then catching them in an agreed format. Any objects of similar size can be used, including stones and shells, although in the ancient world, and still in some parts of the world today, a particular bone from hooved animals, the talus bone or astralagus, can be used, hence the game name of 'knucklebones'. A knucklebone could also be used as a form of dice, although the sides were not numbered, each of the four long sides having a different shape.

The ancient Greek version of this game (*Astrgaloi*) used a set of four bones, and it is probable that it spread to Rome and Roman soldiers in turn brought the game to Britain. Within the collections at the British Museum is a statue called 'The Knucklebone Player', which dates to around AD 150 and depicts a young woman or nymph playing with knucklebones. The game, or variations of it, remained popular in the medieval period, portrayed in Pieter Bruegel the Elder's painting *Children's Games* (1560), and is still played today.

There are several Victorian, blue-glazed ceramic examples on the database (for example, HAMP-30B569 and YORYM-56B28E and LANCUM-A84751) which were also used in games of this type.

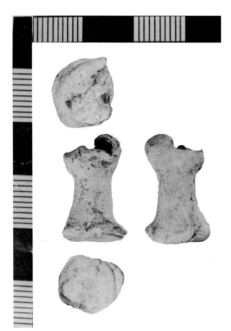

Above: Ceramic glazed blue gaming piece, *c.* AD 1850–1950, dimensions 16.1 mm x 17.1 mm x 17 mm. Object (YORYM-56B28E) is an almost identical piece. (HAMP-30B569)

Left: Lead gaming piece. (NLM-76C011)

43. China marble (LON-72AAE9)
Post-medieval (AD 1840–80)
Found at Southwark, London. Diameter 20.60 mm, weight 10.70 g
Identified and recorded by Stuart Wyatt.

The marble illustrated here dates to the mid-nineteenth century (1840–80) and is decorated with two different hand-painted flower or 'pinwheel' motifs, either side of a set of parallel pink lines around the middle of the marble. China marbles with hand-painted flower or geometric designs, glazed and unglazed, were popular from the mid-nineteenth century into the early twentieth century.

Marble games have a long history and although often made of clay or glass, any spherical object (olives, nuts, small pebbles) could have been used by children at any time. One of the earliest sets of marbles often cited is a group found accompanying an Egyptian child who was buried around 3000 BC. The Roman poet Ovid describes various marble-type games using nuts and there is an image of Roman children playing a marble-type game on the side of a sarcophagus (British Museum object number 1865,0103.7). Until the

Ceramic painted marble. (LON-72AAE9)

Above: Mixed group of ceramic and glass marbles, including some Codd's bottle stoppers (post-AD 1870), *c.* 1840–1970. (NLM-8FC67E)

Left: Polished stone marble with initials 'B B', post-medieval, diameter 17.66 mm. (LON-E162BE)

seventeenth century marbles of stone or clay were common, although glass marbles had been hand-made in Venice and Bohemia since the fifteenth century. Some of the oldest marbles found in Britain are a group of clay marbles dating from 1547 to 1558 that had been concealed during renovations at Coventry Free Grammar School. It wasn't until the 1890s that machine production of glass marbles began, although this ceased in Britain during the First World War, leading to a boom in production in the United States and the eventual domination of glass marbles over their ceramic counterparts.

Chapter 8
Other Finds from Childhood

This section brings together an assortment of childhood-related objects recorded by the PAS that either do not easily fit into one of the previous categories, or do not occur in sufficient range to qualify as a separate chapter of their own.

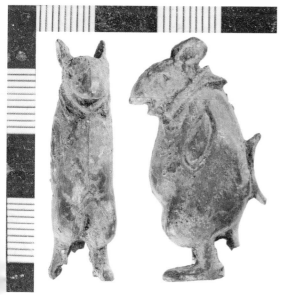 

Above left: Lead-alloy mouse figurine, 35 mm high. This is one of the Cadbury's 'Cococubs' figurines, a set of thirty-two hollow-cast, hand-painted miniature animals that were a promotional gimmick by Cadbury's Bournville in the 1930s. Designed by the artist and children's writer Ernest Aris and manufactured by the toy company Britains, they proved to be a huge publicity success. (NLM-DB506B)

Above right: 'Cococub' mouse figurine. (Image author's collection)

44. Copper-alloy socketed arrowhead (DUR-E3B3AB)
Bronze Age (1000–800 BC)
Found at Malton, North Yorkshire. Length 48.48 mm, weight 9.8 g
Identified and recorded by Sara Gibson.

Evidence for children in the Bronze Age, as in the whole of prehistory, is elusive and largely comes from burials. This copper-alloy arrowhead or spearhead is a rare find in Britain and is a particularly small example. Miniature or small-scale does not however equate to being intended for use with or by children and the small socket diameter of this object could also indicate a ceremonial function. Miniature socketed axeheads also have an uncertain function. Based on Bronze Age full-size versions, they appear to date from the Bronze Age through to the Roman period, as with the two objects illustrated here.

Copper-alloy
socketed
arrowhead.
(DUR-E3B3AB)

Late Bronze Age to Roman copper-alloy miniature socketed axehead, *c.* 1150 BC–AD 410, length 26.69 mm, weight 12.39 g. (WILT-6FB3B4)

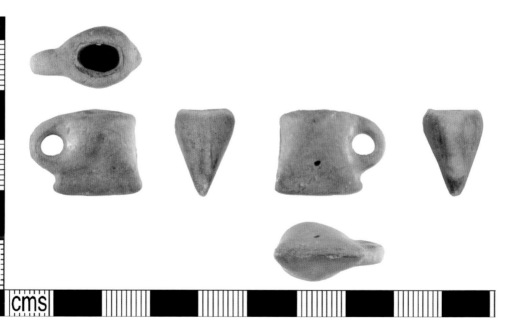

A complete copper-alloy Bronze Age to Roman miniature socketed axehead, *c.* 2350 BC–AD 410, probably a votive offering, length 15.33 mm, weight 7.91 g. (WILT-923994)

45. Putto figurine (BERK-3D408B)
Roman (AD 43–410)
Found at Cox Green, Windsor and Maidenhead. Height 47.1 mm, weight 40.9 g
Identified and recorded by Philip Smither with Martin Henig.

A putto (plural putti) is a small figurine of a naked infant boy, sometimes winged, the word putto deriving from the Latin word *putus* (boy). Several putti have been recorded by the PAS, and this particular figurine depicts the boy infant holding a ball, as does another from Lincolnshire (LIN-A7D5D9), and both feature Romano-British influences. Putti are often shown playing with animals, as in this winged figurine where he is holding a goose (BERK-B60E47). Figurines of this type seem to be found at or near religious sites but could equally have been used in household shrines to the gods. They are not the same as Cupid figurines, which tend to be more slender, older youths than the infants depicted by putti. An example from Surrey shows some similarities with Cupid figurines but is fuller-bodied and wingless (SUR-CE0231). Putti occur not just as figurines but are also portrayed on other materials, for example, on decorated Samian pottery where they are again often depicted playing. During the Renaissance period, putti re-appear in artwork and are the predecessor of the modern boy-like Cupid so familiar on Valentine's Day cards.

mm The British Museum's Portable Antiquities Scheme

Incomplete copper-alloy figurine of a boy, Romano-British. (BERK-3D408B)

A complete copper-alloy figurine of a winged boy seated with his arms around the neck of a goose, Romano-British, *c.* AD 43–200, height 59.9 mm. (BERK-B60E47)

Copper-alloy figurine of a boy in running pose, *c.* AD 43–410, height 60.96 mm. (SUR-CE0231)

46. Handcuffs (LVPL-D988AE)
Modern (AD 1780–1900)
Found at Stockport. Length 61.8 mm, weight 39.8 g
Identified and recorded by Steven Groves.

These handcuffs are small enough to have been for use with a child, but in this instance, as they were made from copper alloy rather than of iron, it is thought that they are more likely to have been for use in play. Although modern laws dictate children under eighteen are tried and sentenced differently to adults, this has not always been the case. In the eighth century AD children aged ten and over who were found guilty of crimes could expect to be handed the same sentences as adults, including the death penalty, although in the tenth century King Athelstan raised the age to twelve. Even in the eighteenth century children as young as fourteen faced the very real prospect of transportation to the British colonies. The later nineteenth and twentieth centuries saw a number of changes regarding how children were treated by the courts, and in 1948 the placement of under seventeens in adult prisons ended.

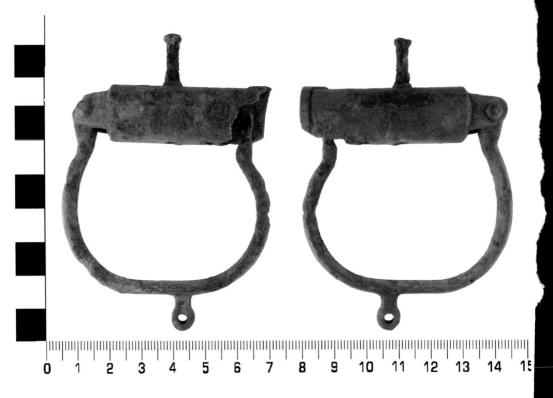

Small copper-alloy handcuffs. (LVPL-D988AE)

47. Silver-gilt apostle spoon (LVPL-883FF2)
Post-medieval (AD 1500–1660)
Found at Bassetlaw, Nottinghamshire. Length 32.01 mm, weight 10.9 g
Identified and recorded by Teresa Gilmore.

This object is a silver-gilt finial from an Apostle spoon. A silver spoon given as a christening gift is still a commonplace practice today, yet the tradition started back in the sixteenth century. During the fifteenth century spoons depicting the Apostles were used at the table, but in the sixteenth century it became popular to give a single spoon or a set of these spoons as a baptismal present. A full set depicting the twelve Apostles, sometimes with the addition of a thirteenth spoon, known as the master spoon, was the most extravagant gift. Four spoons of the Evangelists were another option, or, depending on the wealth of the

Silver-gilt finial from an Apostle spoon. (LVPL-883FF2)

Complete silver-plated copper-alloy spoon with moulded terminal representing an Apostle, *c.* AD 1600–1800, length 108.46 mm. (WAW-0B5D78)

godparent, just a single spoon of the saint matching the child's name could suffice. Each Apostle is shown with a trait that defines them, for example a sword or a key for St Peter, a bag of money for Judas. The most expensive were made in silver, such as the example here, although cheaper versions were also made in copper alloy (for example, SUR-672327). Many were melted down during the Reformation and the silver re-used, although a full set can be seen in the British Museum (object number 1981,0701.2). During the Victorian period many replicas were made, including miniature versions.

The full set of Apostle spoons and their associated symbols are:

The Master (Jesus): a cross and orb
St Peter: a sword or a key
St Andrew: a cross
St James the Greater: a pilgrim's staff
St James the Lesser: a fuller's bat
St John: the cup of sorrow
St Philip: a staff
St Bartholomew: a knife
St. Thomas: a spar
St Matthew: an axe
St Jude: a carpenter's set square
St Simon: a long saw
Judas: a bag of money

48. Toy sword mould (HESH-87A116)
Post-medieval (AD 1500–1650)
Found at Hampton Bishop, Herefordshire. Length 88.3 mm, weight 246.47 g
Identified and recorded by Peter Reavill.

This carved stone fragment, as one half of a two-piece mould, provides evidence for the manufacture of toys, which from the thirteenth century were made by casting copper and lead-alloy metals. There are two designs carved into the surface of this mould, a highly decorated sword pommel, handle and handguard, with a smaller design tentatively identified as a possible chape for a scabbard to use with the sword. The overall design of the sword places this mould in the sixteenth century, when compared stylistically to full-sized swords of the period. Generally toy edged weapons such as swords and daggers are rare finds, with one possible sword guard recorded (from Surrey SUR-D3B4BC). Moulds used in the production of miniatures are rare, with this example and one dated to the fifteenth century used to produce miniature jugs, the only two known from England.

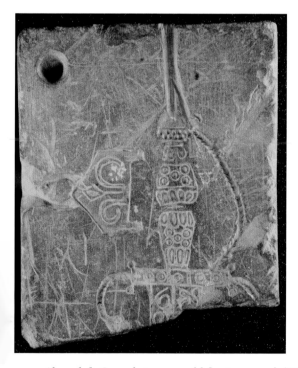 

Above left: Carved stone mould for toy sword. (HESH-87A116)

Above right: Mould for production of miniature metal jugs. (Copyright acknowledgement to Herefordshire Museum Service)

49. Boy Scouts badge (NLM-750B64)
Modern (AD 1920–60)
Found at Grasby, East Midlands. Height 22 mm, weight 3.24 g
Identified and recorded by Martin Foreman.

In 1908 Robert Baden-Powell (later Lord) published *Scouting for Boys*, a year after taking a group of boys camping on Brownsea Island. So successful was this publication that it led to the formation of the Boy Scouts Association in 1910. Originally aimed at boys aged between eleven and eighteen, more children wanted to join, hence the creation in 1916 of the Wolf Cubs (now Cubs) for those aged between eight and eleven, and subsequent sections for other age groups. A separate organisation, the Girl Guides, was established by Baden-Powell and his sister to provide activities that were deemed more suitable for girls at the time. Classed as a voluntary group, the scouting movement's military background, through Baden-Powell's army service, was utilised during both world wars as Scouts undertook various National Service roles. In 1991 girls were allowed to join all sections of the Scouts, while previously (from 1976) this had been restricted to girls aged between sixteen and twenty.

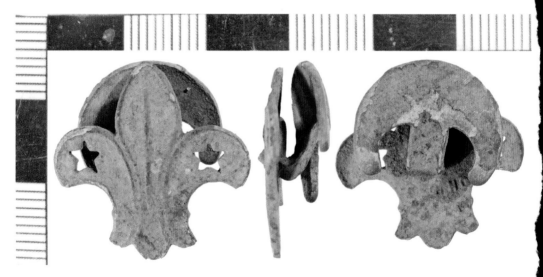

Boy Scouts badge, possibly a type given to adults who were not Scout leaders, for example, group secretaries. (NLM-750B64)

50. Bobby Bear Club badge (PUBLIC-8184F2)
Modern (AD 1930–35)
Found near Caistor, Lincolnshire. Diameter 25 mm, weight 7.17 g
Identified and recorded by Bob Garlant.

While there are no teddy bears on the database, there is this Bobby Bear Club badge. The badge dates to the 1930s with an image based on the popular Steiff bear, first sold in the early 1900s. From the 1920s–60s children's characters were a popular feature in newspapers, which often resulted in the creation of membership clubs which produced annuals and other memorabilia.

In 1919 the London-based *Daily Herald* newspaper started printing the Bobby Bear comic strips (pre-dating Rupert Bear, who was first published in 1920). The Bobby Bear Club was set up in 1930 and was free to join if you collected enough newspaper coupons. By 1932 there were some 400,000 members, who on joining each received a special booklet, a membership card and a yearly birthday card. Alongside the Bobby Bear Club, other examples include Pip, Squeak and Wilfred and The Teddy Tail Club.

Bobby Bear Club badge.
(PUBLIC-8184F2)

Bobby Bear Club membership
certificate, 1935. (Image author's
collection)

Sources

Online Blogs and Collections

The Motherhood in Prehistory Blog: https://motherhoodinprehistory.wordpress.com/

Roman families on Hadrian's Wall: https://www.vindolanda.com/blog/roman-women-and-children-part-4

Museum of London: https://www.museumoflondon.org.uk/discover/feeding-babies-roman-london

Pollock's Toy Museum: https://www.pollockstoymuseum.co.uk/

Dolls Houses Past and Present: https://www.dollshousespastandpresent.co.uk

Young V&A Museum and online collection: https://www.vam.ac.uk/young

Society for the History of Childhood and Youth: https://shcydigitalchildhoods.org/dir/

Books

Carroll, Maureen, *Infancy and Earliest Childhood in the Roman World: 'a Fragment of Time'* (Oxford University Press, 2018)

Forsyth, Hazel and Egan, Geoff, *Toys, Trifles and Trinkets; Base-metal miniatures from London 1200-1800* (Museum of London, 2005)

Nowell, April, *Growing Up in the Ice Age: Fossil and Archaeological Evidence of the Lived Lives of Plio-Pleistocene Children* (Oxbow Books, 2021)

Orme, Nicholas, *Medieval Children* (Yale University Press, 2003)